Workplace Wellness

Real Stories, Real Solutions

Shruti Dey

Workplace Wellness

Real Stories, Real Solutions

Table of Contents

Word of Thanks

This book is a testament to the many incredible people I've been privileged to meet throughout my life, each of whom has contributed to my growth, both personally and professionally.

To my husband, Mr. Rajeev Kumar Dey, who encouraged me to begin this journey, thank you for your unyielding support, love, and faith in my vision. This book would not have been possible without you by my side.

My heartfelt gratitude to my brother, Mr. Ishank Jain, who has always believed in my abilities and championed my dreams. Your unwavering faith and support have been a powerful force, and I am forever grateful.

To my parents, who taught me the importance of resilience, compassion, and integrity, thank you for your boundless love and support. You are my foundation, my guiding light, and my greatest teachers.

I also owe a deep gratitude to my aunt Ms. Veena Bala Jain and my mentors across various workplaces, whose wisdom and guidance helped me build both competence and confidence. Your mentorship was invaluable in shaping the professional I am today. To every person I have met along my journey, those who offered a fresh perspective, taught me a lesson, or simply listened—I am grateful. Each interaction has left an imprint, adding to the understanding and empathy that fill these pages. This book is a humble tribute to each of you who believed in me, taught me something valuable, or simply walked with me for a while on this path. Thank you for being part of my journey.

Introduction

A Journey Through Corporate Corridors

Before I became a mental health professional, I spent over a decade as a Human Resources (HR) professional, working within the walls of various corporate environments. My role was more than just recruiting, handling payroll or training and development; it involved closely observing people and the complexities of their experiences at work. I met employees who carried burdens that no one saw, and I listened to stories of stress, anxiety, and personal struggles that unfolded quietly, often away from the limelight. It was in these moments, sitting across from someone who was just trying to hold it all together, that I began to understand the importance of mental health in the workplace.

In HR, I saw firsthand how often mental health was overlooked and how employees were expected to compartmentalize their personal struggles. People were praised for "powering through" or labeled as "strong" for showing up to work despite personal or professional turmoil. But I couldn't shake the feeling that there had to be a better way to handle these situations. I began asking myself: *What if we could address these struggles openly? What if the workplace itself became a supportive environment where people didn't have to hide their stress and anxieties?*

As I worked with teams and supported individuals facing different types of challenges, my sensitivity toward mental health grew stronger. I saw how quickly burnout could set in, how hard it was for someone to admit to feeling overwhelmed, and how few people knew where to turn for support. My interest in mental health took root here, and it ultimately became my calling.

The Shift from HR to Mental Health

Transitioning from HR to a mental health professional wasn't a straight path, but it felt natural. As I gained experience in counseling and life coaching, I found myself particularly drawn to helping people navigate workplace issues. Over the years, I've worked with countless individuals struggling with work-related stress, burnout, imposter syndrome, relationship conflicts, and more. This work has taught me that mental health challenges are deeply personal, yet they're also universal—especially when it comes to the workplace.

In writing this book, I wanted to create a resource that could help professionals like you manage these challenges more effectively. I believe that our careers should not come at the expense of our well-being, and I want to help readers understand that it's possible to thrive at work without sacrificing mental health.

Why This Book?

This book is a collection of stories and lessons, each reflecting a common workplace mental health struggle. I've drawn from real-life scenarios (disguised to protect confidentiality) as well as composite characters inspired by countless individuals I've worked with. Through these stories, I hope to show you that you're not alone in your experiences. Whether you're dealing with imposter syndrome, burnout, workplace conflicts, or the pressure to perform, each chapter is designed to offer practical insights and strategies that you can apply to your own life.

Unlike many self-help books that focus only on individual resilience, this book takes a broader approach. It recognizes the role that workplace culture, management, and societal expectations play in our mental well-being. While building personal resilience is important, it's equally essential to understand and address the external factors that contribute to our mental health challenges.

What You'll Find Inside

Each chapter in this book follows a specific workplace issue, illustrated through a story that many of you may find familiar. From the ambitious employee struggling with burnout to the isolated remote worker and the professional facing bias or imposter syndrome, the stories in this book span the range of issues faced by modern workers.

After each story, I've included practical advice, reflections, and exercises to help you process and address similar challenges. These tools are designed to be easily incorporated into your daily life, whether you're looking to reduce stress, improve your work-life balance, or build stronger connections with your colleagues.

This book is for anyone who wants to cultivate mental well-being while still advancing in their career. It's for high achievers, for steady performers, for those just starting their careers, and for those considering a career change. Most of all, it's for people who understand that mental health and professional success are not mutually exclusive.

A Note to the Reader

I hope this book serves as a supportive companion on your journey to a healthier, more fulfilling work life. If you've ever felt alone in your struggles or unsure of how to address the challenges you face at work, know that this book is here for you. It's my heartfelt contribution to a more mentally healthy and supportive workplace culture, a place where each of us can bring our best selves to work without compromising our well-being.

Thank you for allowing me to be part of your journey. Let's take this step together, toward a workplace where success and mental health go hand in hand.

Chapter 1: Recognizing the Signs

Story of Aarav

Aarav was known around the office as the "go-to guy." As a senior project manager in his company's marketing department, he was always juggling multiple projects, delivering presentations, and stepping in to help his teammates whenever they needed support. Aarav's calendar was consistently packed with meetings, and his emails seemed to pile up faster than he could respond. His colleagues admired his dedication, and his managers appreciated his commitment. Aarav seemed to thrive under pressure.

But something had changed. Over the past few months, Aarav had started experiencing exhaustion that didn't go away with a good night's sleep. His mornings felt heavier, and he'd find himself hitting the snooze button multiple times, something he never used to do. Aarav began noticing a persistent headache that would linger through the day, and his concentration would drift mid-meeting. His once bright ideas now felt forced, and his patience—something he'd prided himself on—seemed to be running thin. The turning point came one evening when, after yet another long day at work, Aarav found himself snapping at his wife over a trivial matter. Her concerned look made him pause. For the first time, Aarav acknowledged that he was overwhelmed. This wasn't just regular stress; it was something deeper, something that seemed to have seeped into his everyday life, affecting not just his work but also his personal relationships.

Understanding Chronic Stress and Burnout

Aarav's experience is a common story, especially among high achievers who are driven by ambition and a commitment to their careers. It's easy to attribute these feelings to a "busy period" or a need to work harder. But when stress becomes a constant in one's life, it can slowly build up, leading to burnout—a state of emotional, physical, and mental exhaustion that can have serious repercussions on both personal and professional well-being.

Chronic stress often creeps in gradually. Early signs may be subtle: feeling tired even after sleeping, trouble focusing, a loss of patience, or perhaps a decline in job satisfaction. As it progresses, it can manifest in physical symptoms like headaches, muscle tension, and digestive issues. Left unchecked, chronic stress can evolve into burnout, a state of complete emotional depletion where motivation and enthusiasm vanish. Burnout doesn't just affect productivity; it impacts overall mental health and personal relationships. Recognizing these early signs is essential to preventing burnout and ensuring a balanced, healthy approach to work.

Practical Tips for Recognizing and Managing Chronic Stress

1. **Self-Assessment Check-Ins**

   Regularly checking in with yourself is an important first step in managing stress. Take a few moments each week to ask yourself:

   - Am I feeling more tired than usual?

   - Am I enjoying my work as much as I used to?

   - Are my personal relationships suffering because of my work demands?

   These small reflections can help you catch patterns that may indicate chronic stress before it escalates.

2. **Prioritizing and Setting Boundaries**

   One of the key contributors to chronic stress is an overwhelming workload. Learn to set realistic boundaries by:

   - Saying no to additional tasks when you're already stretched thin.

   - Setting specific work hours and sticking to them.

   - Prioritizing tasks based on urgency and impact, focusing on what truly requires your attention.

3. **Mindfulness and Stress-Reduction Techniques**

   Practices like mindfulness, deep breathing, and progressive muscle relaxation can reduce stress in the moment and over time. Mindfulness, for example, involves focusing on the present moment without judgment, which helps you manage thoughts that may be contributing to your stress.

4. **Seeking Support and Talking About It**

   Chronic stress can often feel isolating, especially when you think others expect you to keep up appearances. Opening up to someone—a friend, family member, or counselor—can be a powerful way to process what you're feeling and gain perspective.

5. **Physical Activity and Sleep Hygiene** Engaging in physical activity, even for a short time each day, can help manage stress hormones and improve mood. Similarly, practicing good sleep hygiene—going to bed at the same time, limiting screen time before bed, and creating a restful environment—can improve sleep quality, which in turn supports mental resilience.

Reflection and Exercise

Take a moment to reflect on how often you experience stress in your work life. Jot down the signs that resonate with you—whether it's physical symptoms like headaches or emotional signs like irritability. Next, identify one small change you could make this week to manage that stress, whether it's setting a boundary, practicing mindfulness, or reaching out to a friend.

Take Away

Aarav's story is a reminder that success doesn't have to come at the cost of your well-being. Recognizing the early signs of stress and burnout is the first step toward creating a more balanced and fulfilling work life. Small changes—whether in perspective, habits, or boundaries—can go a long way in ensuring that your career brings joy and satisfaction, not exhaustion.

Chapter 2: The Silent Struggler

Story of Meera

Meera had always been a diligent worker. After graduating with a degree in marketing, she landed a stable job at a mid-sized firm, where she was initially excited about her role. She appreciated the security that came with her position and the routine it provided. However, as the months turned into years, Meera began to feel a growing sense of discontent.

Despite doing her job well, Meera felt an emptiness creeping in. The tasks that once sparked her enthusiasm had become mundane, and she struggled to find motivation. Each morning, she would drag herself out of bed, knowing the day ahead would be filled with repetitive meetings and the same projects. While her colleagues engaged in lively discussions about promotions and new projects, Meera often felt like a bystander in her own life.

Her evenings were filled with thoughts of "What if?" What if she had pursued her passion for graphic design? What if she had taken that risk to start her own business? As these questions flooded her mind, she felt more trapped in her current situation. Despite her outward appearance of stability, inside, Meera was a silent struggler, grappling with a sense of unfulfillment that weighed heavily on her.

One evening, while scrolling through social media, Meera stumbled upon a post that read, "Don't let fear of failure keep you from pursuing your dreams." Those words resonated with her. It was time to confront her feelings and assess what was holding her back.

Recognizing the Signs of Unfulfillment

Meera's story is a common one. Many individuals experience periods of unfulfillment in their careers, often without fully recognizing the signs. Feelings of stagnation, lack of enthusiasm, and a desire for change can indicate that it's time to evaluate one's career path and make adjustments.

Identifying the root causes of unfulfillment is the first step towards addressing them. It's important to acknowledge feelings of dissatisfaction rather than brush them aside. By doing so, individuals can take proactive steps toward creating a more fulfilling professional life.

Practical Tips for Addressing Lack of Motivation and Purpose

1. **Self-Reflection and Assessment**
   Take time to reflect on your career journey. What aspects of your job do you enjoy? What do you find draining? Writing these thoughts down can help clarify your feelings and guide your next steps.

2. **Set Personal Goals**
   Establish short-term and long-term goals that align with your passions. Whether it's pursuing a new skill, networking, or considering a job change, setting clear objectives can reignite your motivation.

3. **Explore New Opportunities**
   Don't be afraid to seek out new projects or responsibilities within your current job. Volunteering for a cross-departmental project can expose you to different roles and may help you discover new interests.

4. **Seek Support and Mentorship**
   Connect with colleagues, friends, or mentors who can provide insights and guidance. Sharing your feelings with others can often lead to new perspectives and encouragement.

5. **Consider Professional Development**
   Look into courses, workshops, or certifications that align with your interests. Investing in your development can help you gain new skills and open doors to opportunities you may not have considered.

Reflection and Exercise

Reflect on your current job and your feelings about it. Write down three things you enjoy about your work and three aspects that you find unfulfilling. Consider one small action you can take this week to address these feelings—whether it's reaching out to a mentor, exploring a new project, or starting a course.

Take Away

Meera's journey illustrates that unfulfillment can be a signal for change rather than a reason for despair. By recognizing the signs and taking proactive steps, it's possible to cultivate a more satisfying and meaningful career. Remember, it's never too late to pursue your passions and redefine your path.

Chapter 3: Overcoming Imposter Syndrome

Story of Nikhil: A Rising Star Plagued by Self-Doubt

Nikhil joined his new company with a mix of excitement and nerves. As a fresh hire in the competitive world of marketing, he knew he had the skills and qualifications. After all, he graduated with honors and had previously interned at reputable firms. But as he started receiving positive feedback and even a few accolades in his new role, a feeling of unease began to creep in. Despite being recognized for his contributions, Nikhil found himself questioning his abilities and worth, believing he was "fooling" everyone and would soon be "found out." He felt like a fraud.

Nikhil's feelings escalated as he started comparing himself to his colleagues. He couldn't help but feel that his achievements were more luck than skill, and he feared that any day now, someone would see through his "act." Whenever his manager praised him, Nikhil brushed it off, thinking, "If only they knew how clueless I really am." His anxiety around being exposed as an "imposter" intensified to the point that it started affecting his productivity and mental well-being. He was constantly worried, second-guessing every move and rereading every email before hitting send.

To avoid what he perceived as inevitable failure, Nikhil began to avoid taking on new responsibilities. Instead, he played it safe, choosing tasks he knew he could handle easily. In meetings, he would shy away from offering ideas, fearing they wouldn't be "good enough." Over time, this pattern of avoidance and self-doubt led Nikhil to feel isolated and dissatisfied, despite his role being everything he had hoped for professionally. Something needed to change.

Understanding Imposter Syndrome

Nikhil's story is one that many high-performing individuals face, yet few openly discuss. Imposter syndrome is characterized by persistent self-doubt, a feeling that one's successes are not deserved, and a fear of being exposed as a "fraud." Common among high achievers, it creates a cycle where individuals discount their accomplishments, attribute their success to external factors like luck, and constantly feel that they're "faking it."

The irony is that imposter syndrome often appears in individuals who are, in fact, skilled and competent. Studies suggest that perfectionists, high achievers, and those who receive significant praise at work are particularly vulnerable. This self-doubt can lead to burnout, low job satisfaction, and even missed opportunities as individuals hold themselves back to avoid "exposure."

Imposter syndrome isn't a formal diagnosis but rather a mental pattern. It exists on a spectrum, and anyone experiencing it should be aware that it's possible to reduce its impact and develop a stronger sense of self-assurance.

Strategies to Overcome Imposter Syndrome

While overcoming imposter syndrome is challenging, adopting specific strategies can make a difference. Here's a guide to help individuals like Nikhil develop self-acceptance, confidence, and internal validation:

1. **Acknowledge Your Feelings**
   Recognizing and accepting imposter feelings is the first step toward overcoming them. Instead of dismissing your achievements or doubting their authenticity, validate your feelings without letting them define you. Remind yourself that self-doubt is a common experience, especially when stepping into new roles or high-stakes situations.
2. **List Your Accomplishments and Skills**
   Create a "brag book" or a list of your professional achievements and skills. Revisit this list whenever imposter feelings arise. Regularly reminding yourself of your accomplishments helps counterbalance the tendency to dismiss your achievements. Nikhil, for instance, could make a list of all the projects he successfully completed, the accolades he received, and the positive feedback from his colleagues and managers.
3. **Seek Constructive Feedback**
   Ask for honest, constructive feedback from trusted colleagues or mentors. This will give you an objective perspective on your performance. Often, our inner critic exaggerates our weaknesses

while ignoring strengths. By seeking feedback, you'll receive a balanced view, helping you see yourself more accurately.

4. **Avoid Comparisons**

   Comparing yourself to others is a surefire way to fuel imposter syndrome. Instead, focus on your own growth and set personal goals. Remember, everyone is on a unique journey with different strengths and challenges. Nikhil can remind himself that his path doesn't have to mirror anyone else's and that his achievements stand on their own.

5. **Practice Self-Compassion**

   Treat yourself with the same kindness and understanding that you would offer a friend. Self-compassion involves acknowledging your struggles without harsh self-criticism. When Nikhil feels inadequate, he can remind himself that it's okay to be imperfect and that everyone experiences moments of self-doubt.

6. **Reframe Negative Thoughts**

   Challenge and reframe negative self-talk. For example, instead of thinking, "I don't know what I'm doing," Nikhil could reframe this as, "I'm still learning, and it's okay to ask for help." By shifting his internal dialogue, he can gradually weaken the power of imposter thoughts and build a more positive self-image.

7. **Celebrate Small Wins**

   Rather than focusing solely on big achievements, celebrate the small successes along the way. By acknowledging progress in everyday tasks, you'll cultivate a habit of seeing your efforts as valuable. Nikhil could take time at the end of each week to reflect on the tasks he accomplished, no matter how minor they may seem.

Reflections and Exercises

1. *Reflection Exercise: Ask yourself, "What are my three most significant achievements?" Write these down in detail, and reflect on the skills and efforts required to achieve them. Recognize that these accomplishments were not accidental.*

2. ***Daily Affirmation****: Every morning, repeat a simple affirmation such as, "I am skilled, I am capable, and I am worthy of my success." This reinforces a positive mindset and creates a habit of self-assurance.*

3. ***Visualization****: Visualize a future scenario where you are confident, composed, and successful in a challenging situation. Imagine feeling at ease, sharing your ideas, and receiving positive feedback. Visualization can help shift your mental state and increase your confidence over time.*

Nikhil's Journey to Self-Acceptance

As Nikhil began incorporating these practices, he noticed a gradual shift in his mindset. By celebrating small wins and accepting praise instead of deflecting it, he started to build genuine confidence in his abilities. In time, he was able to take on more challenging tasks without the crippling fear of "being exposed." Rather than shrinking back, Nikhil began to participate in meetings, contribute ideas, and even offer guidance to new colleagues, realizing that his knowledge and skills were not only valid but also valuable.

Instead of waiting to "feel" like he belonged, Nikhil learned that the key to overcoming imposter syndrome lay in practicing self-compassion, embracing his strengths, and continually growing. His journey wasn't one of eliminating self-doubt but rather learning to move forward with it. Through this, he became an example to his peers of resilience and the power of self-belief.

Key Takeaways

- Imposter syndrome is common among high achievers and can be managed by changing the way we perceive and validate ourselves.

- Self-acceptance and constructive self-reflection are critical in overcoming the fear of being "found out."

- Building internal validation, practicing self-compassion, and celebrating small wins are valuable practices in developing authentic confidence.

In addressing imposter syndrome, we must remember that our growth doesn't hinge on perfection or complete certainty. Instead, it flourishes when we allow ourselves the grace to be learners, embrace our imperfections, and recognize the worth that we bring to our roles.

Chapter 4: Navigating a Toxic Workplace

Story of Priya: Thriving Despite a Toxic Culture

Priya joined a high-profile real estate firm with excitement and high expectations. She was passionate about her work and thrilled to be part of a company known for its impressive client roster. However, the reality of the company's culture soon began to unravel.

Within her first month, Priya noticed the competitive atmosphere was more cutthroat than collaborative. Colleagues regularly undermined one another, and any errors—no matter how minor—were seized upon and highlighted. Her manager, Rajesh, was known for a "sink or swim" philosophy, giving feedback that was harsh and personal rather than constructive. Team meetings often felt like battlefields, where criticism was harsh, and acknowledgment of accomplishments was rare.

Initially, Priya tried to stay positive, reminding herself that her hard work would be recognized eventually. But the constant negativity began to weigh heavily on her. She felt anxious every morning and dreaded work. Even when she took a break, her mind buzzed with thoughts about upcoming deadlines or potential criticisms. She realized that her work stress was seeping into her personal life, affecting her relationships and sleep quality. Eventually, Priya recognized she was dealing with a toxic work environment and decided to take proactive steps to manage her well-being.

Understanding a Toxic Workplace

A toxic workplace is an environment that significantly impacts employees' emotional, mental, and even physical health due to pervasive negativity, lack of support, and unhealthy practices. Common signs of a toxic workplace include:

1. **Poor Communication**: Inconsistent messaging, unclear expectations, and lack of constructive feedback.

2. **Micromanagement**: Managers who control every aspect of their team's tasks, leaving little room for autonomy.

3. **Lack of Recognition**: Little to no acknowledgment of accomplishments, with emphasis placed only on mistakes.

4. **Gossip and Backstabbing**: An atmosphere where employees are encouraged to compete or talk negatively about one another.

5. **High Turnover Rates**: Frequent departures of employees, as toxic environments are unsustainable in the long term.

These characteristics create high levels of stress and anxiety and can lead to burnout, low morale, and a breakdown in trust among team members.

For employees like Priya, navigating such a workplace can become an emotionally taxing experience that may affect not only their productivity but also their self-worth.

Strategies to Manage and Mitigate Toxicity

1. **Set Boundaries**
   Maintaining personal boundaries is essential. Priya learned to limit her interactions with toxic colleagues and prioritize tasks that didn't require collaboration with negative team members. Setting boundaries helps create a buffer, protecting one's mental and emotional energy from unnecessary stress.

2. **Focus on Personal Growth**
   Instead of letting the toxic culture define her, Priya focused on her own professional growth. She enrolled in an online course related to her field and attended workshops outside of work. By focusing on skill-building, she shifted her energy away from the negativity surrounding her.

3. **Seek Out Positive Allies**
   Finding like-minded colleagues who share similar values can be incredibly helpful in a toxic workplace. Priya discovered a few co-workers who felt the same way about the environment and began spending time with them. These allies provided a sense of camaraderie, allowing her to feel less isolated.

4. **Document Your Work**
   In a toxic workplace, it's wise to keep a record of your contributions and achievements. Priya started documenting her

projects and accomplishments, giving her tangible evidence of her worth, which helped counteract any undermining she faced.

5. Consider Professional Support

Seeking support from a counselor or therapist can be beneficial when dealing with a toxic work environment. Therapy provided Priya with tools to manage her emotions and reinforced her confidence, empowering her to maintain her sense of self-worth.

Reflections and Exercises

- **Journal Exercise**: Reflect on the toxic behaviors you've observed and how they affect you. Write about three specific ways you can create boundaries to protect your energy.

- **Affirmations**: Every day, remind yourself, "I am here to do my best. I am not defined by the behaviors of others."

Moving Forward: Thriving Despite the Negativity

For Priya, finding her voice and setting boundaries within a toxic environment became empowering. She became more resilient, learning to separate her self-worth from her job and recognizing the power of personal agency. Ultimately, these experiences helped her understand the importance of prioritizing mental health over professional gains, guiding her to seek healthier workplaces.

Chapter 5: Handling Micromanagement

Sunita's Story: Striving to Breathe Under the Weight of Control

Sunita was thrilled to land her new role as a project manager in a reputable IT company. A hard worker and a natural leader, she was looking forward to making a real impact with her fresh ideas and problem-solving skills. However, her excitement was short-lived as she quickly encountered a major roadblock—her manager, Arvind.

Arvind was a perfectionist, known for his "hands-on" approach. He wanted to be involved in every decision and required constant updates on all tasks. At first, Sunita thought his attention to detail was a sign of his commitment to quality, but she soon realized it was more than that. Arvind would dictate the exact steps she should take, review her emails before sending, and often redo her work himself. He would call her at odd hours, send her reminders about even minor tasks, and expect immediate responses to his messages.

What had initially seemed like close supervision quickly became suffocating. Sunita began doubting her capabilities, wondering if her manager's constant hovering was a reflection of her competence. Her enthusiasm faded, and she felt her creativity and confidence slowly eroding. She even hesitated to offer new ideas, fearing they would be criticized or dismissed outright.

As months passed, Sunita found herself feeling trapped and anxious at work. She dreaded Arvind's calls and emails, and the micromanagement became so pervasive that she began to lose motivation. She even questioned if her job was worth the mental toll it was taking on her well-being.

Understanding Micromanagement

Micromanagement, while often rooted in a desire for quality control, tends to have negative effects on employees' productivity, confidence, and morale. A micromanaging leader can stifle creativity, erode trust, and create a work environment where employees feel they have little autonomy or ownership of their work. Some common signs of micromanagement include:

1. **Excessive Oversight:** Managers needing constant updates on every small task, even when it's unnecessary.

2. **Reluctance to Delegate**: Managers often don't trust team members to take full responsibility, redoing work themselves or making all decisions.

3. **Control over Minor Details:** A focus on dictating not just what needs to be done but exactly how to do it.

4. **Constant Monitoring**: Frequent check-ins and communication to the point of disrupting workflow.

5. **Lack of Trust:** The underlying message is that the manager doesn't trust the employee's judgment or capability.

Micromanagement is a symptom of deeper issues—either a lack of trust in employees, a need for control, or perhaps even the manager's own insecurity about performance. While it may temporarily ensure work is done as per a manager's standards, in the long run, it leads to disengagement, lowered morale, and high turnover.

Sunita's Strategy to Cope and Grow

Sunita recognized that she had two options: continue feeling stifled or try to improve her situation. Here are the steps she took to address the micromanagement issue:

1. **Self-Reflection and Awareness**

   Sunita realized she was experiencing micromanagement and its impact on her confidence. She assessed what specific aspects of her job were most affected, like her decision-making and autonomy. She recognized the negative toll on her well-being, which motivated her to address the issue.

2. **Open Communication**

   After much thought, Sunita scheduled a meeting with Arvind. Instead of pointing out his micromanaging behavior, she framed the conversation around her professional development. She expressed her eagerness to take on more responsibility and emphasized her commitment to meeting his expectations. She asked for more autonomy on small tasks and offered to provide regular updates to ensure he felt informed. This allowed her to request more freedom in a non-confrontational way.

3. Proactive Transparency

To build Arvind's trust, Sunita proactively shared her project progress through weekly summaries. This way, Arvind received updates without needing to intervene constantly. By anticipating his concerns and addressing them upfront, she could subtly ease his need for control.

4. Building Credibility and Trust

Sunita focused on excelling in her tasks, delivering high-quality work consistently. By demonstrating her competence and reliability, she hoped to gradually earn Arvind's trust. Over time, as he saw her efficiency and dedication, he began to reduce his oversight slightly.

5. Setting Boundaries

While she initially felt intimidated, Sunita also set small boundaries around her work hours and responses to minor requests outside of working hours. She gradually taught Arvind that she could be relied on to deliver quality work without his constant input.

Takeaways from Sunita's Story

Sunita's journey is an example of finding ways to cope with and navigate micromanagement rather than surrendering to it or feeling trapped. Here are some broader takeaways for readers dealing with micromanagement:

1. Identify the Root Cause

Recognizing why a manager may be micromanaging (such as lack of trust or their own insecurities) can help employees approach the issue with empathy and a strategic mindset.

2. Set Boundaries Politely

It's essential to establish boundaries around personal time and task ownership. Politely letting a manager know when you need space to complete your work or requesting fewer interruptions can gradually help reduce micromanagement.

3. Showcase Reliability

Demonstrating consistent, high-quality performance can help build trust, gradually shifting the manager's perception and possibly easing their need to control.

4. Offer Solutions

Engaging in open, solutions-focused conversations with the manager, like Sunita did, can open up a pathway for greater autonomy while still showing respect for the manager's position.

5. Focus on Growth

Even in a micromanaged environment, focusing on skill-building and personal development helps maintain confidence and resilience, making it easier to pursue other opportunities if necessary.

Final Reflection

Sunita's experience highlights that, while micromanagement can feel limiting, there are ways to strategically work around it. Taking steps to communicate, showcase competence, and set boundaries can help regain some autonomy and mitigate the negative impacts. Ultimately, Sunita's journey encouraged her to focus on her long-term growth and made her a stronger, more resilient professional.

Chapter 6: The Loneliness of Remote Work

Story of Raj: Finding Connection in a Virtual World

Raj, a vibrant marketing specialist in his early 30s, thrived in office environments. A natural extrovert, he relished the daily energy boost he received from impromptu hallway chats, brainstorming sessions, and shared coffee breaks. For Raj, working wasn't just about completing tasks; it was about the camaraderie, mutual support, and encouragement he found in being part of a team.

When his company transitioned to remote work, Raj was hopeful about the flexibility it would bring, looking forward to a home setup that he imagined would give him more freedom. However, as weeks turned into months, the effects of working alone began to weigh on him. Raj missed the synergy of a bustling office and the motivation that came from his teammates' energy. The isolation slowly ate away at his enthusiasm, and tasks that once seemed easy now felt overwhelmingly tedious.

The virtual team meetings did little to alleviate his loneliness. Conversations were scheduled, stiff, and often felt transactional—lacking the warmth of a casual chat in the break room or the supportive atmosphere of an in-person brainstorming session. While his manager would regularly check in on project progress, Raj found himself hesitant to share how he was truly feeling about the isolation. He worried that talking about it might be seen as a lack of resilience or professionalism. Instead, he internalized his struggles, feeling disconnected not only from his team but also from the company culture he once felt so aligned with.

To combat this, Raj began taking deliberate steps to create a sense of connection and community within his remote setup. He organized virtual coffee breaks with colleagues to bring back the small, everyday conversations he missed. These informal catch-ups created space for more relaxed, friendly chats, allowing him to bond with his teammates beyond project deadlines and work-related updates. Slowly, this simple change brought a sense of relief, breaking up the monotony of solitary workdays.

In addition to his virtual coffee breaks, Raj joined some of the company's online social groups and events, including a wellness group and a Friday book club. This gave him more opportunities to interact with colleagues he didn't usually work with directly, broadening his social circle within the company and bringing back some of the shared company culture he missed so much. It reminded Raj that he wasn't alone in feeling isolated and helped him rediscover a sense of connection and purpose.

Raj also noticed the impact of a structured routine on his mental well-being. He committed to starting and ending work at specific times and dressed for work as if he were going to the office. This discipline helped him create boundaries between work and home life, giving him back a sense of normalcy and routine he had lost in the remote setup.

Understanding Remote Work Isolation

Remote work isolation has affected millions of professionals who once relied on social interaction as part of their work experience. Working from home offers flexibility but often comes at the cost of reduced human connection. Unlike office environments where spontaneous exchanges occur naturally, remote work can be rigid, with interactions often limited to scheduled meetings and emails. This lack of casual contact can lead to feelings of loneliness, reduced motivation, and decreased productivity.

In Raj's case, the isolation stemmed from the absence of his typical support system—the casual yet vital social connections that fueled his creativity and gave him purpose. Without regular face-to-face interactions, Raj initially found himself adrift, feeling disconnected from his team and struggling with a sense of loneliness. He eventually learned that, in a virtual world, building connections requires deliberate effort and a willingness to adapt.

Strategies to Cope with Remote Work Isolation

1. **Establish Virtual Connections**
   Raj initiated regular check-ins with his teammates, even if they were just short video calls. By reaching out, he recreated a sense of camaraderie and connection. Informal conversations can help bridge the gap created by physical distance, fostering a virtual support network.

2. **Create a Structured Routine**
    Working remotely often leads to blurred boundaries between work and personal life. Raj developed a structured daily routine, which included designated breaks and a consistent start and end time. This structure gave him a sense of normalcy and stability, helping him stay focused and balanced.

3. **Engage in Social Activities Outside of Work**
    Recognizing that his social needs weren't being met solely through work, Raj made an effort to join online hobby groups and attend virtual meet-ups. He discovered that these connections helped alleviate his loneliness and provided a sense of community.

4. **Practice Self-Care**
    Spending long hours at home can lead to fatigue and burnout. Raj incorporated self-care practices into his daily routine, including regular exercise, meditation, and screen breaks. Prioritizing his well-being allowed him to recharge and maintain his motivation.

5. **Consider a Change of Scenery**
    Occasionally, Raj worked from a local coffee shop or co-working space. A change of environment broke the monotony, giving him a refreshing shift in perspective and reducing the isolation of working alone at home.

Reflections and Exercises

- **Gratitude Exercise**: Each day, write down one positive interaction you've had, even if it's a virtual one. This practice will help you stay connected with the supportive relationships in your life.

- **Affirmation**: "I am connected, valued, and capable of fostering meaningful relationships, regardless of the distance."

Takeaways from Raj's Story

Raj's journey offers valuable insights for anyone navigating the challenges of remote work isolation:

1. **Intentional Connection is Key**

   In remote settings, creating relationships requires intention. Virtual coffee breaks or unstructured video calls can recreate some of the casual interactions that are often missing, helping combat isolation and maintain team spirit.

2. **Engagement Beyond Work Tasks Builds Community**

   Participating in online social groups, wellness activities, or interest-based clubs within the company provides a space for interaction beyond immediate work needs, enhancing the sense of belonging.

3. **Structured Routines Help Maintain Balance**

   Setting up a routine and dedicated workspace can recreate the structure of an office, making it easier to separate work from personal life and maintain productivity.

4. **Open Communication with Supervisors is Crucial**

   Talking openly with managers about struggles with remote work isolation can lead to supportive adjustments, such as additional check-ins or group meetings, fostering a more connected team environment.

5. **Prioritizing Self-Care and Mental Health**

   Incorporating mental health practices—like meditation, exercise, or hobbies—helps maintain a positive mindset and reduces stress, reinforcing resilience in a remote setting.

6. **Professional Networks Provide Additional Support**

   Connecting with people in similar roles or industries outside the immediate company can provide a valuable support system, offering fresh perspectives and reducing feelings of isolation.

By taking these steps, Raj was able to overcome the emotional challenges of remote work and find connection in a digital world, showing that even when working remotely, it's possible to build a fulfilling work life with intentional action and a commitment to well-being. His story is a reminder that while remote work may feel isolating, meaningful relationships and support are within reach if we make the effort to connect, even in virtual ways.

Chapter 7: Work-Life Balance for Parents

Story of Anjali: Juggling Career and Family Life

Anjali is a manager at a fast-paced tech firm and the mother of two young children, ages 3 and 6. She loves her job, finding it both rewarding and intellectually stimulating, but she also feels deeply committed to her role as a mother. Anjali is constantly balancing between deadlines and dinner, client calls and school pickups, and late-night reports and bedtime stories.

Her day often starts before sunrise, with a few moments to herself for exercise or meditation. But as the house comes to life, her focus shifts to preparing breakfast, packing lunches, and getting the kids ready for school. Amid the morning rush, she mentally organizes her tasks for the workday, all the while feeling the strain of a packed schedule. Despite these efforts, there are often moments when she's frazzled by the competing demands of her dual roles as a parent and a professional.

Anjali has worked hard to set up systems that allow her to manage both family and work. She's meticulous with her schedule, organizing her calendar to accommodate work meetings, family obligations, and even "quiet time" blocks for uninterrupted focus. Still, even with the best-laid plans, there are days when a sick child, a late client call, or a work deadline requires her to rethink everything. The unpredictability sometimes leaves her feeling like she's falling short in both arenas.

One particular evening, Anjali was faced with a critical deadline on a high-stakes project that required her immediate attention. She tried her best to manage her time during the day, squeezing in work during her lunch break and staying a few hours longer than usual. However, when she finally arrived home, her daughter looked up at her with disappointment. She had promised to attend her daughter's school play that evening, and in her efforts to balance her work responsibilities, she had completely forgotten. The guilt she felt was overwhelming, and it lingered even after she finished her work.

Recognizing that her approach wasn't sustainable, Anjali decided to seek guidance from a career coach who specialized in work-life balance strategies. The coach introduced her to a few practical tools and strategies, which Anjali slowly implemented over time:

1. Prioritization and Flexibility

The coach encouraged Anjali to focus on prioritizing high-impact tasks and to practice flexibility. Instead of viewing her roles as rigid, the coach suggested that Anjali approach each day with an adaptable mindset. She also learned the importance of identifying non-negotiable priorities for both her family and her work.

2. Setting Boundaries and Communicating Needs

Anjali also worked on setting clearer boundaries with her colleagues and her family. For instance, she would block off specific "no-meeting hours" where she focused solely on her children, and she became more vocal about her availability at work. By communicating her needs transparently, she found that her colleagues were surprisingly supportive and often adapted schedules to ensure her workload was manageable.

3. Self-Care and Delegation

Self-care became a non-negotiable for Anjali, with daily walks, reading time, and even the occasional weekend break. Additionally, she learned to ask for help, both at home and work. She began delegating tasks at work to her junior team members, giving them learning opportunities while also creating more breathing room for herself. At home, she organized support from family members and occasionally hired a babysitter for nights when work ran late.

Over time, Anjali noticed that these changes were making a tangible difference. By giving herself permission to occasionally step back and seek support, she found renewed energy and a more harmonious balance. She was able to be fully present at home, enjoying her time with her children without worrying about unfinished work. Conversely, at work, she approached her projects with a clearer head and greater efficiency, knowing that she had support when things got tough.

Understanding the Challenges of Work-Life Balance for Parents

The struggle to balance career and family life is familiar to many working parents. The expectations can be overwhelming, and it's easy to feel caught between competing responsibilities. While societal pressures often place high expectations on parents to "have it all," achieving a true balance requires realistic expectations, clear communication, and practical strategies to navigate the daily challenges.

Anjali's story highlights a few universal challenges faced by working parents, including guilt, the unpredictability of family needs, and the pressure to excel in both personal and professional roles. However, her journey also shows that achieving a balanced life doesn't necessarily mean doing everything perfectly; rather, it involves a willingness to adapt, seek support, and practice self-compassion.

Strategies for Maintaining Work-Life Balance as a Parent

1. **Set Boundaries for Work and Family Time**
   Anjali learned the importance of setting boundaries to separate her work hours from family time. By designating specific hours for each, she could focus fully on one area without feeling guilty about neglecting the other.
2. **Prioritize Self-Care and Rest**
   She realized that taking care of her own well-being was essential for being able to care for her family and manage her job. Scheduling short breaks and committing to self-care practices, such as meditation or exercise, helped her recharge and approach both roles with more energy.
3. **Involve Family in Daily Routines**
   Anjali began involving her children in daily chores and routines. This not only made tasks more manageable but also helped her spend quality time with them while teaching them responsibility.

4. **Seek Support and Communicate Needs**
   Anjali opened up to her manager about her situation and was pleasantly surprised by the support she received. She was able to adjust her hours slightly to allow for better balance, and her manager respected her need for flexibility.

5. **Let Go of Perfectionism**
   By accepting that she didn't need to be perfect in every role, Anjali found relief from the self-imposed pressure. Focusing on being

"good enough" allowed her to celebrate her efforts and cherish moments with her family without feeling guilty about work.

Reflections and Exercises

- **Reflection Prompt**: List three ways you can set boundaries between work and family life to reduce stress and increase quality time with both.

- **Affirmation**: "I am doing my best, and my best is enough for myself and my family."

Takeaways from Anjali's Story

1. Prioritize and Focus on High-Impact Activities

Recognize that not all tasks are equally important, both at work and at home. By identifying the high-impact activities and focusing on them, it becomes easier to achieve meaningful results without feeling overwhelmed.

2. Set Boundaries with Intentionality

Clear boundaries are essential in maintaining a work-life balance. Defining specific work hours, "no-meeting times," or days reserved for family commitments can help prevent burnout and enhance productivity.

3. Communicate Openly and Advocate for Flexibility

Open communication with colleagues, supervisors, and family members can foster understanding and allow for greater flexibility. By voicing one's needs and priorities, it's often possible to create a supportive environment that accommodates both professional and family responsibilities.

4. Embrace Delegation and Support Systems

Delegating tasks at work and involving family members in household responsibilities can lighten the load and make balancing work and family life more manageable.

5. Practice Self-Care Regularly

Taking care of personal well-being is essential to prevent burnout. Even small routines, like daily exercise, moments of quiet, or time for personal hobbies, can provide a much-needed mental and emotional boost.

6. Acknowledge and Accept Imperfection

No one can do it all, and striving for perfection can lead to unnecessary stress. Accepting that some days may be more challenging than others can allow parents to approach their roles with grace and flexibility.

Anjali's experience emphasizes that work-life balance is a dynamic process, with each day requiring a renewed effort to balance personal and professional demands. However, by approaching each challenge with adaptability and the right tools, parents can find ways to be present, productive, and fulfilled in both areas of their lives.

Chapter 8: Dealing with Job Insecurity

Story of Manav: Coping with Uncertainty in the Workplace

Manav had been with his company, a well-established manufacturing firm, for nearly seven years. During this time, he had seen both highs and lows in the industry, but nothing quite as challenging as the downturn that began last year. News of layoffs circulated frequently in the office, and each time an email arrived from HR, it felt like an ominous reminder of the uncertainty hanging over everyone's heads.

As a diligent employee, Manav had always gone the extra mile for his team, contributing long hours and consistently meeting his targets. Despite his strong performance, he found himself questioning whether his job was truly secure. With a young family to support and a home loan, the thought of losing his job was frightening. He began to experience sleepless nights, his mind cycling through worst-case scenarios. It wasn't long before this stress started to affect his productivity and his relationships with both colleagues and family members.

One morning, after hearing that a close friend and coworker had been let go, Manav felt a surge of anxiety that he struggled to hide. His manager noticed the tension and invited him for a coffee chat. During their conversation, Manav expressed his fears, admitting how the job uncertainty was affecting his focus and confidence. His manager, who had also been feeling the strain of the downturn, offered some guidance. She suggested that he consider building his skills in areas that were critical to the company's evolving strategy and to start creating a professional network outside of his current role.

Taking his manager's advice to heart, Manav began to explore ways to enhance his resilience in the face of uncertainty. He enrolled in a few online courses in emerging fields within his industry, dedicating a few hours each week to broaden his skill set. This gave him a sense of control, even when he couldn't control the broader industry dynamics. In parallel, he started connecting with other professionals on LinkedIn and attending industry networking events. These activities not only helped him grow his confidence but also made him feel more prepared to adapt to potential changes, even if they weren't in his immediate company.

Manav also began practicing mindfulness and stress management techniques. He'd read about the benefits of mindfulness in reducing anxiety and found that a few minutes of deep breathing exercises during his work breaks helped him stay present and grounded. His evenings became a time to focus on quality family moments, which reinforced a sense of stability and support in his life.

As time went on, Manav found himself better equipped to handle the stress of job insecurity. While the layoffs continued, he felt less overwhelmed by fear and more motivated to be proactive. By focusing on what he could control—his skills, network, and mental well-being—Manav discovered that he could build resilience even in uncertain times. Eventually, the company stabilized, and although Manav's role remained secure, he knew that he had cultivated skills and confidence that would help him face any future uncertainties head-on.

Understanding Job Insecurity and Its Impact

Job insecurity is an increasingly common concern in today's fast-paced work environment, particularly in industries vulnerable to economic changes. For employees like Manav, the constant fear of losing one's livelihood can take a toll on mental health, impacting both personal and professional life. Studies have shown that job insecurity can lead to increased anxiety, depression, and reduced productivity. When employees feel uncertain about their future, they may also struggle to fully engage in their roles, creating a cycle that perpetuates the fear of being let go.

Manav's story illustrates the psychological impact of job insecurity and the ways in which proactive steps can mitigate the effects of this fear. By focusing on skill-building, networking, and self-care, Manav developed tools to maintain his well-being, proving that resilience is achievable even in times of heightened uncertainty.

Strategies to Manage Job Insecurity

1. **Develop a Contingency Plan**
   Manav began creating a financial safety net by saving a portion of his income each month. Having an emergency fund provided him

with a sense of security and reduced his anxiety over potential job loss.

2. **Enhance Your Skill Set**

    By taking courses to enhance his skills, Manav became more adaptable and marketable. He started updating his resume, making sure it reflected his achievements and skills, which helped boost his confidence.

3. **Seek Mentorship and Advice**

    Manav sought advice from a mentor who had gone through a similar experience. This guidance gave him a realistic perspective and helped him make informed decisions about his career path.

4. **Maintain a Positive Mindset**

    Practicing gratitude and focusing on what he could control helped Manav stay positive. He acknowledged his fears but didn't let them dictate his outlook or behavior at work.

5. **Expand Your Network**

    Networking both within and outside of his industry provided Manav with new opportunities and connections, making him less dependent on his current role and more resilient against job loss.

Reflections and Exercises

- **Journal Exercise**: Write down three actions you can take to prepare for job insecurity, focusing on what you can control rather than what's uncertain.

- **Affirmation**: "I am adaptable, resourceful, and capable of handling any career challenge that comes my way."

Takeaways from Manav's Story

1. **Focus on Building Transferable Skills:** Enhancing one's skills can be an effective way to gain confidence during uncertain times. By investing in areas that are in demand, employees can increase their marketability and feel more prepared for any future career transitions.

2. **Expand Your Professional Network:** Building connections outside of one's immediate workplace can be invaluable in creating future opportunities. Engaging with industry professionals, attending events, and leveraging online platforms like LinkedIn can make employees feel less isolated and better supported.

3. **Practice Mindfulness and Stress Management:** Taking care of mental health is crucial when dealing with job insecurity. Techniques such as mindfulness, deep breathing, and regular physical exercise can help alleviate anxiety, allowing individuals to stay focused and grounded.

4. **Create a Safety Net and Financial Plan**: Financial planning is essential to feeling secure in uncertain times. Establishing an emergency fund, cutting unnecessary expenses, and having a backup plan can ease some of the stress associated with job insecurity.

5. **Embrace Adaptability and Resilience:** Job insecurity can be an opportunity to develop resilience and adaptability. By cultivating a growth mindset and being open to learning, individuals can better navigate changes in their industry and feel more equipped to handle challenges.

6. **Set Boundaries and Focus on Quality Time with Family**: Maintaining a strong support system can provide comfort during uncertain periods. Spending quality time with family and friends can help reinforce a sense of stability and reduce the feeling of isolation that job insecurity often brings.

Manav's experience serves as a reminder that while job security may fluctuate, one's response to it can be steady. By taking actionable steps to manage both professional and personal areas of life, employees can create a sense of security and confidence that extends beyond their current role.

Chapter 9: The Challenges of Career Stagnation

Story of Kavita: Rediscovering Motivation in a Stagnant Role

Kavita was once the rising star of her company. She had started in an entry-level role in her early 20s and climbed her way up through hard work, dedication, and a deep commitment to her field. But now, over a decade later, Kavita felt like she'd hit a wall. While she had accumulated skills and experience, her role had become repetitive, her responsibilities predictable. It was a far cry from the fast-paced learning environment that had initially excited her about the job.

Day by day, Kavita's motivation began to wane. Her workdays felt longer, and her engagement levels dropped. She noticed herself going through the motions without the same enthusiasm. Every attempt to discuss her career path with her supervisor seemed to end in vague assurances rather than concrete steps toward advancement. She watched as some of her younger colleagues quickly advanced, bringing new ideas and fresh perspectives, while she felt her potential and contributions were being overlooked. With every passing month, her feelings of frustration deepened, making her question her value in the workplace.

One afternoon, during a coffee break with her friend and colleague Riya, Kavita shared her feelings of stagnation. Riya listened intently, offering support and understanding. She suggested that Kavita consider reaching out to a mentor within or outside the organization—someone who could offer guidance on navigating the feeling of career plateau. This was an idea Kavita hadn't considered before. The next day, she connected with an industry mentor she admired on LinkedIn and set up an introductory call.

During their conversation, her mentor provided invaluable insight: career growth isn't always linear, and sometimes a plateau can be an opportunity to expand one's expertise in other directions. Inspired by this perspective, Kavita started researching areas that could enhance her current role and make her contributions feel more valuable. She found that developing skills in project management and digital tools could not only help her in her current job but also make her a stronger candidate for future roles.

Over the next few months, Kavita enrolled in online courses for project management and data analysis, dedicating a few hours each week to upskilling. She began to incorporate these new skills into her daily tasks, managing projects more efficiently and even suggesting improvements in processes that impressed her team. Gradually, her confidence returned, and her contributions were noticed. Eventually, Kavita's supervisor offered her a project lead role on a high-visibility initiative, which aligned with her newly developed skills.

With a renewed sense of purpose, Kavita found that the sense of career stagnation had transformed into a period of growth and self-investment. She realized that while external recognition is important, the commitment to personal growth, even during seemingly stagnant periods, can bring fulfillment and open doors to new opportunities. By shifting her mindset and taking proactive steps, Kavita found her career's momentum again, on her own terms.

Understanding Career Stagnation

Career stagnation can occur when employees feel they're not advancing or growing in their roles. This plateau can create feelings of frustration, low motivation, and self-doubt, especially in individuals who are used to consistent career progression. Like Kavita, many professionals find themselves in this position at some point in their careers. While it's easy to view stagnation negatively, it can also be a chance for self-reflection, skill-building, and reassessment of one's career goals.

Kavita's journey demonstrates that overcoming career stagnation often requires a shift in mindset and a willingness to adapt. By identifying areas where she could enhance her skills and add value to her current role, she not only improved her job satisfaction but also opened up new avenues for advancement. Her story is a reminder that growth can be self-directed and that career fulfillment often comes from a proactive approach to personal development.

Strategies to Overcome Career Stagnation

1. Set New Goals

Kavita set personal goals to challenge herself within her current role. This gave her a renewed sense of purpose and direction, even in a familiar environment.

2. **Expand Your Skills**
   By taking up new responsibilities, Kavita learned new skills and increased her value to the team. She enrolled in relevant courses that kept her engaged and provided growth, regardless of her official position.

3. **Network and Seek Mentorship**
   Networking helped Kavita gain insights into other career paths and allowed her to connect with potential mentors. These connections provided guidance and motivated her to keep pursuing growth.

4. **Look for Lateral Opportunities**
   Kavita explored lateral moves within her organization to gain different experiences. This broadened her skill set, adding variety and reducing her feelings of stagnation.

5. **Consider Long-Term Career Development**
   By setting long-term career goals, Kavita regained motivation. She visualized where she wanted to be in the future and worked towards it, even if her current role was only a stepping stone.

Reflections and Exercises

- **Reflection Prompt**: Reflect on your career path and list three areas where you would like to grow. Identify specific actions to achieve these goals.

- **Affirmation**: "I am capable of creating my own growth and finding purpose in my work."

Takeaways from Kavita's Story

1. **Seek Mentorship**: When feeling stuck, reaching out to a mentor can provide new perspectives and guidance. A mentor can offer insights into how to navigate career plateaus, suggesting approaches or skills to explore that may not be immediately obvious.

2. **Reframe Stagnation as an Opportunity**: Career stagnation can be reframed as a period for self-development rather than a dead end. By using this time to acquire new skills, employees can create opportunities for growth and add value to their roles, positioning themselves for future advancement.

3. **Focus on Skill-Building and Self-Investment**: Enrolling in courses, attending workshops, or seeking certifications relevant to one's role can enhance skill sets, making employees feel more engaged and capable of contributing meaningfully to their teams. Continuous learning not only breaks the monotony but also builds confidence and expertise.

4. **Develop a Growth Mindset:** Shifting from a fixed mindset, which sees career progression as a straight path, to a growth mindset can help professionals view career stagnation as a temporary phase. With a growth mindset, individuals focus on self-improvement and embrace the idea that skills can be developed and that new opportunities can arise at any time.

5. **Engage in Self-Reflection**: Regularly assessing personal and career goals can help employees stay aligned with their passions and strengths. Self-reflection allows individuals to evaluate their current trajectory and decide if they need to make changes or pursue new directions within or outside their current role.

6. **Celebrate Small Wins and Progress**: Recognizing personal progress, no matter how small, can build motivation and prevent feelings of career dissatisfaction. Celebrating wins along the way, whether a new skill acquired or a project completed, can create a sense of accomplishment and purpose.

Kavita's experience illustrates that while career stagnation can feel frustrating, it is also a time for reassessment and growth. With a proactive approach and a willingness to invest in self-development, anyone can reignite their career, discover new passions, and chart a path toward a more fulfilling professional life.

Chapter 10: Overcoming Creative Burnout

Story of Rhea: Rekindling Passion Amid Creative Exhaustion

Rhea had always been known for her creativity. As a graphic designer at a well-regarded advertising agency, her work had been featured in high-profile campaigns, and her fresh ideas had often set her apart. But after several years in the industry, Rhea felt an inexplicable weariness. Deadlines felt tighter, and her once-energizing brainstorming sessions now felt like a drain. Where she once saw a canvas for endless creativity, she now saw a series of tasks and obligations. Each time she sat down to create, her mind felt blank—a heavy silence where ideas once flowed freely. She knew she was burning out, but didn't know how to address it.

Adding to her struggles was the ever-present pressure to meet the agency's high standards. Her manager frequently reminded her that "clients expect the best," and, slowly, the joy of designing became a burden. Rhea felt like she was constantly chasing perfection, unable to produce work that felt authentic to her creative spirit. She began to question her career choice, wondering if she'd lost her passion for design altogether.

In an attempt to recharge, Rhea took a week off, but the days passed without any noticeable change in her mood. She tried to spark inspiration by scrolling through portfolios of other designers online, but the comparison left her feeling more inadequate and uninspired. One evening, during a conversation with her friend Maya, a writer who had also experienced burnout, Maya suggested a different approach. "Maybe it's not just about taking time off. Maybe you need to reconnect with why you started creating in the first place."

Maya's words struck a chord. That weekend, Rhea decided to step away from her usual digital tools and explore a more tactile approach to art. She bought a sketchbook, a set of colored pencils, and spent the day at a local park. Away from the pressures of work and client expectations, Rhea let her hand flow freely, sketching whatever came to mind. She drew without a goal, rediscovering the pure joy of creation she had loved as a child. It was the first time in months that she felt genuinely connected to her art.

Inspired by this experience, Rhea began to make it a regular practice. On weekends, she set aside time to create without any digital screens or deadlines. She experimented with watercolor, doodled in her sketchbook, and even tried sculpting with clay—activities that didn't demand perfection but simply allowed her to explore. She also began journaling about her creative journey, noting how different mediums and environments made her feel. Slowly, she noticed a shift: her burnout was lessening, and her enthusiasm for design was returning.

Over time, this personal exploration impacted her work at the agency as well. Rhea brought a fresher perspective to her projects, with ideas that felt authentic and energized. She also became more vocal about setting realistic expectations with clients, suggesting longer timelines for more meaningful creative development. This shift not only improved her mental health but led to more innovative and impactful campaigns that her clients appreciated.

Through reconnecting with her creative roots, Rhea realized that burnout wasn't just about overwork; it was about losing sight of one's passion and purpose. Her journey taught her that nurturing creativity requires not only time but also space to explore without pressure. By taking control of her creative process and finding balance, Rhea rekindled her passion and found a renewed sense of purpose in her career.

Understanding Creative Burnout

Creative burnout often arises when individuals in creative roles feel drained, uninspired, and disconnected from their work. Unlike physical exhaustion, creative burnout can be subtle, building over time as the pressure to deliver high-quality work on demand stifles the natural flow of creativity. For many professionals, including artists, writers, and designers like Rhea, creative burnout can leave them questioning their passion, abilities, and even their career choices. Understanding the underlying causes of creative burnout, such as perfectionism, unrealistic expectations, and lack of rest, is key to preventing and addressing it.

Rhea's experience illustrates that the path to overcoming creative burnout is rooted in rediscovery. Taking time to explore art forms and activities outside her usual work helped her reconnect with the joy of creation. Her story is a reminder that nurturing creativity involves more than meeting deadlines and producing work—it requires space, self-compassion, and, most importantly, a love for the process.

Strategies to Overcome Creative Burnout

1. **Prioritize Rest and Recovery**
   Rhea scheduled regular breaks to recharge, ensuring she wasn't overloading herself. Taking time off helped her approach projects with a fresh mind and reduced her stress.
2. **Explore Creative Hobbies**
   Outside of work, Rhea pursued creative hobbies like painting and photography. Engaging in new forms of art allowed her to reconnect with her creativity in a relaxed environment.
3. **Set Boundaries for Creative Projects**
   By setting realistic boundaries, Rhea avoided taking on excessive work. She communicated her needs to her clients, ensuring she had enough time for each project.
4. **Seek Inspiration from New Sources**
   Rhea explored new media and art forms to spark her imagination. Taking inspiration from other fields helped her break through creative blocks and gain fresh perspectives.
5. **Practice Self-Compassion**
   Rhea practiced self-compassion, reminding herself that creativity ebbs and flows. By being kind to herself, she reduced the pressure to be constantly inspired.

Reflections and Exercises

- **Journal Exercise**: Identify a creative hobby you can explore to reignite your inspiration outside of work.

- **Affirmation**: "My creativity is a gift that I nurture and protect."

Takeaways from Rhea's Story

1. **Revisit Your Passion:** When burnout sets in, reconnecting with the reasons you chose your creative field can be incredibly

healing. Engage in creative activities that bring you joy without the constraints of work demands, deadlines, or expectations.

2. **Create Without Pressure:** Give yourself permission to create without judgment or perfectionism. Set aside time for passion projects or personal art, where you can freely explore and make mistakes. This freedom can help you rekindle your love for your craft.

3. **Engage in Mindful Exploration:** Step away from routine digital tools and try new mediums or environments that stimulate creativity differently. Whether it's painting, doodling, or even exploring nature, fresh experiences can bring new inspiration.

4. **Set Boundaries and Manage Expectations:** Communicate realistic timelines and boundaries with clients or managers to reduce pressure. Protecting your creative process not only enhances your well-being but can lead to more innovative and authentic work.

5. **Practice Self-Compassion:** Understand that creativity is not an endless resource; it needs time to recharge. Be gentle with yourself during low-energy periods, acknowledging that it's normal to have fluctuations in motivation.

6. **Take Mini-Breaks and Unplug:** Regular short breaks can prevent the accumulation of stress and help keep creativity flowing. Disconnect from screens and engage in non-work-related activities that relax and refresh you.

7. **Reflect and Journal:** Documenting your creative journey can help you track patterns, triggers, and moments of inspiration. Reflecting on both positive and challenging experiences can provide insights into your process and help you make adjustments.

Rhea's story underscores the importance of finding joy in the creative process. Overcoming creative burnout involves reconnecting with one's passion, exploring without judgment, and setting boundaries to protect the integrity of one's work. By embracing this approach, anyone can learn to nurture their creativity, bringing renewed energy, authenticity, and fulfillment back to their work.

Chapter 11: Balancing Work with Chronic Illness

Story of Varun: Navigating Chronic Illness and a Demanding Career

Varun had always been a high achiever. With an impressive track record in project management, he was known for his dedication and ability to deliver results under pressure. However, his life took a significant turn when he was diagnosed with a chronic illness—an autoimmune condition that would require ongoing treatment and management. Initially, Varun struggled to come to terms with the reality of living with a chronic illness while maintaining his demanding career in a fast-paced tech company.

At first, he tried to carry on as if nothing had changed. He believed that working harder would prove to his colleagues that he was still capable and that he could manage his health alongside his job. But as the weeks went by, the symptoms of his illness began to take a toll on his energy levels and focus. The fatigue was relentless, and there were days when he could barely keep his eyes open during meetings. Despite his efforts to maintain a facade of normalcy, Varun found it increasingly difficult to cope.

Feeling overwhelmed and isolated, Varun hesitated to share his condition with his manager. He worried that revealing his health challenges would lead to judgment or concern about his ability to perform. However, as his health continued to fluctuate, he realized that keeping his illness a secret was only adding to his stress. After much contemplation, Varun decided to have an honest conversation with his manager, Claire.

To his surprise, Claire was supportive and understanding. She encouraged Varun to prioritize his health and suggested implementing flexible working arrangements that could help him manage his workload better. Together, they explored options such as adjusting deadlines, allowing for remote work on particularly tough days, and incorporating regular breaks into his schedule.

With these accommodations in place, Varun slowly began to feel more in control of his life. He learned to set realistic goals and to communicate openly about his limitations, which reduced the pressure he had been placing on himself. Varun also discovered the importance of self-care. He started integrating mindfulness practices into his daily routine—short meditation sessions, gentle yoga, and ensuring he took time for adequate rest.

As Varun became more comfortable advocating for his needs, he also started to engage with his colleagues about his experiences living with a chronic illness. To his relief, he found that many people were more understanding than he had anticipated. Sharing his story not only provided him with a support network but also fostered an environment of empathy and openness within his team.

Over time, Varun's health stabilized, and he learned to manage his career alongside his illness more effectively. He discovered that being honest about his challenges not only helped him find support but also made him a more resilient and resourceful employee. Varun became an advocate for wellness in the workplace, encouraging his team to prioritize their health and well-being as much as their work.

Understanding the Challenges of Chronic Illness in the Workplace

Chronic illnesses can significantly impact a person's professional life, affecting their energy levels, concentration, and ability to manage stress. The stigma around chronic illness often leads individuals to feel isolated, fearing that revealing their condition could harm their careers. Understanding the importance of open communication and support in the workplace can help mitigate these challenges. Employers who foster an inclusive environment can not only support their employees but also enhance productivity and morale.

Varun's journey illustrates the importance of self-advocacy and creating a supportive work culture. By openly communicating about his illness and seeking accommodations, he was able to maintain his professional identity while prioritizing his health. His story serves as a powerful reminder that vulnerability can lead to connection, understanding, and ultimately, resilience.

Strategies for Managing Work with a Chronic Illness

1. **Communicate Needs with Transparency**
   Varun worked with HR to disclose his illness in a way that protected his privacy while allowing him to receive necessary

accommodations, such as flexible hours and the option to work remotely on difficult days.

2. **Set Boundaries and Prioritize Self-Care**
   Varun began pacing himself, taking regular breaks, and saying no to unnecessary meetings or tasks that drained his energy.

3. **Create a Supportive Network**
   He confided in a few trusted colleagues, which helped reduce his stress as he no longer felt isolated. His peers understood his limitations and offered help when he needed it.

4. **Practice Self-Compassion**
   By embracing self-compassion, Varun stopped comparing his current abilities to his pre-diagnosis self. He accepted that it was okay to work at a slower pace when needed.

5. **Organize Work for Maximum Efficiency**
   Varun implemented productivity hacks, such as time-blocking and prioritizing high-energy tasks in the morning when he felt strongest. This allowed him to accomplish more without overexerting himself.

Reflections and Exercises

- **Reflection Prompt**: Identify ways in which you can advocate for yourself in the workplace, especially if you're facing health challenges.

- **Affirmation**: "I am deserving of respect and understanding as I balance my work with my health."

Takeaways from Varun's Story

1. **Prioritize Open Communication:** Sharing your health challenges with your employer or colleagues can lead to understanding and support. Open conversations about chronic illness can reduce stigma and foster a healthier work environment.

2. **Advocate for Yourself**: Don't hesitate to ask for accommodations that can help you manage your workload while dealing with a chronic condition. Flexibility, understanding, and support are essential for maintaining both health and productivity.

3. **Set Realistic Goals:** Adjust your expectations based on your current health status. Focus on manageable tasks and allow yourself grace on days when your condition may hinder your performance.

4. **Incorporate Self-Care Practices**: Engage in activities that promote well-being and reduce stress, such as mindfulness, meditation, and physical exercise. These practices can help you navigate the emotional and physical challenges of chronic illness.

5. **Seek Support**: Build a network of colleagues and friends who understand your situation. Sharing your experiences can create a support system that helps you cope with challenges more effectively.

6. **Educate Others**: Use your experiences to inform and educate your colleagues about chronic illnesses. By raising awareness, you can help create a more inclusive and empathetic workplace.

7. **Embrace Resilience**: Understand that navigating a chronic illness while pursuing a career is a journey that requires adaptability and resilience. Celebrate small victories and recognize the strength it takes to advocate for your needs.

Varun's story highlights the complexities of balancing a chronic illness with a demanding career. Through open communication, self-advocacy, and support, individuals can navigate their challenges while continuing to thrive professionally. His journey is a testament to the power of vulnerability and resilience in the face of adversity.

Chapter 12: Navigating Workplace Bullying

Story of Shalini: Confronting a Hostile Colleague

Shalini had always been a dedicated and hardworking employee in her marketing firm. She was known for her creativity and ability to collaborate effectively with her team. However, her experience took a turn when a new team member, Priya, joined the department. At first, Shalini was excited to work with Priya, who came highly recommended for her skills. But it quickly became evident that Priya had a different approach to teamwork— one that involved undermining others to showcase her own abilities.

Initially, Shalini brushed off Priya's snide comments and passive-aggressive behavior, thinking it was just a phase of adjustment. However, as time went on, Priya's behavior escalated. She frequently criticized Shalini's ideas in meetings, often stealing credit for their collaborative projects and subtly belittling her in front of colleagues. The hostile work environment began to affect Shalini's confidence and motivation. She found herself second-guessing her contributions and dreading team meetings. Feeling increasingly isolated and frustrated, Shalini confided in her close colleague, Raj, who encouraged her to address the situation directly with Priya. Raj explained that confronting the issue head-on might not only improve their working relationship but also help restore Shalini's confidence. Although nervous about the confrontation, Shalini realized she could not continue to let Priya's behavior impact her mental health and job performance.

Shalini decided to request a private meeting with Priya. She prepared herself by jotting down specific examples of Priya's behavior that had made her uncomfortable, focusing on how it affected the team's dynamic rather than attacking Priya personally. During their conversation, Shalini calmly expressed her feelings, explaining how Priya's comments had undermined her confidence and affected their collaboration.

To her surprise, Priya reacted defensively at first, dismissing Shalini's concerns and insisting she was simply trying to push for excellence. However, Shalini maintained her composure, reiterating her intent to foster a positive team environment. She emphasized her desire to work together constructively, and this approach gradually disarmed Priya. By the end of the conversation, Priya agreed to be more mindful of her words and actions moving forward. After their meeting, Shalini noticed a significant change in Priya's behavior. Though not perfect, Priya made an effort to be more collaborative and respectful. Shalini's willingness to confront the situation empowered her and helped rebuild her confidence. Moreover, her proactive approach inspired others in the team to address their concerns more openly, leading to a healthier team dynamic overall.

Understanding Workplace Bullying

Workplace bullying can manifest in various forms, including verbal abuse, exclusion from team activities, and undermining of one's work. It creates an environment where employees feel anxious, undervalued, and unable to perform at their best. Understanding the dynamics of workplace bullying is essential in fostering a respectful work environment where everyone feels safe to express their ideas and concerns.

Shalini's experience highlights the importance of addressing bullying behavior directly. By confronting Priya in a constructive manner, she was able to initiate a change in their working relationship. This illustrates that while confronting bullying can be intimidating, it is often necessary for personal and professional growth.

Strategies for Handling Workplace Bullying

1. **Document Incidents Thoroughly**
   Shalini began keeping a detailed record of each incident, including dates, times, and witnesses. This provided her with evidence if she needed to report the behavior.
2. **Set Boundaries and Assert Yourself**
   She practiced assertiveness techniques, calmly but firmly addressing her colleague when they crossed a line. By not reacting emotionally, she maintained control of the situation.
3. **Seek Support from Supervisors or HR**
   Shalini approached HR with her documented incidents and explained the impact of her colleague's behavior on her work. HR initiated an investigation, leading to a resolution that improved the work environment.
4. **Find Allies and a Support Network**

By building a network of supportive colleagues, Shalini created a buffer against her bully's tactics. These allies boosted her confidence and reassured her that she wasn't alone.

5. **Practice Self-Care to Manage Stress**
Shalini engaged in self-care practices, such as mindfulness and journaling, to process her feelings and reduce the stress caused by bullying.

Reflections and Exercises

- **Journal Exercise**: Write about an experience where you felt bullied or undermined at work and how you handled it.

- **Affirmation**: "I am worthy of respect, and I will stand up for myself with confidence and integrity."

Takeaways from Shalini's Story

1. **Recognize the Signs of Bullying**: Understand what constitutes bullying in the workplace, including passive-aggressive behavior, undermining comments, and isolation tactics. Awareness is the first step toward addressing the issue.

2. **Document Specific Incidents**: Keep a record of bullying behaviors and their impact on your work. This documentation can be valuable if you choose to escalate the issue to a supervisor or HR.

3. **Communicate Effectively**: When addressing a hostile colleague, focus on how their behavior affects you and the team. Use "I" statements to express your feelings without assigning blame.

4. **Seek Support:** Confide in trusted colleagues who can provide perspective and advice. They may have experienced similar situations and can offer valuable insights.

5. **Practice Self-Advocacy**: Don't hesitate to stand up for yourself. Confronting bullying behavior can empower you and improve your self-confidence.

6. **Promote a Positive Culture**: Encourage open communication within your team. When employees feel comfortable sharing their concerns, it fosters a supportive work environment.

7. **Know When to Escalate**: If the bullying behavior persists despite your efforts to address it, consider involving a manager or HR. Your well-being and mental health should always be a priority.

Shalini's story illustrates that confronting workplace bullying can lead to positive changes, not only for oneself but for the entire team. By taking action, she not only stood up for herself but also contributed to creating a more respectful and collaborative workplace environment.

Chapter 13: Coping with Constant Change

Story of Rohit: Adapting to a Rapidly Changing Workplace

Rohit had always prided himself on being adaptable. As a mid-level manager in a tech company known for its innovation and fast-paced environment, he had navigated through several projects that required him to shift his strategies quickly. However, the recent organizational restructuring sent shockwaves through the company, resulting in a series of rapid changes that left Rohit feeling overwhelmed.

The company's leadership decided to implement a new software system designed to streamline operations, but the transition was poorly managed. Employees were given minimal training, and deadlines were moved up without consideration for the team's capacity. Rohit found himself in the difficult position of having to support his team while also adjusting to the new system himself. He noticed his team was increasingly stressed and frustrated, struggling to meet their targets while trying to learn the new software on the fly. As the weeks went by, Rohit felt the weight of the situation pressing down on him. He began to experience symptoms of anxiety, struggling to sleep at night and feeling irritable during the day. He was concerned that if he didn't address these changes effectively, the morale of his team would plummet, leading to decreased productivity and higher turnover.

Determined to navigate through this tumultuous period, Rohit scheduled a team meeting to address the challenges they were facing. He encouraged open communication, allowing team members to voice their concerns about the new software and the unrealistic deadlines. Rohit listened carefully, validating their feelings and assuring them that it was okay to struggle with the changes.

In response to the team's concerns, Rohit took the initiative to reach out to upper management, advocating for additional training sessions and a more realistic timeline for implementing the new system. He proposed the idea of buddy systems within the team, pairing those who had a better grasp of the software with those who were struggling. This approach fostered a sense of teamwork and support, enabling colleagues to learn from one another.

Additionally, Rohit introduced weekly check-ins to monitor progress and address any lingering issues. These meetings allowed the team to celebrate small wins and provided a platform for ongoing feedback, creating a sense of camaraderie during a challenging time. Rohit also made a point to practice self-care, setting aside time each day for physical activity and mindfulness, which helped him manage his anxiety and maintain a positive outlook.

As a result of these efforts, the team began to adapt more smoothly to the changes. Their productivity improved, and the atmosphere shifted from one of frustration to one of collaboration and support. Rohit learned that while change can be daunting, fostering open communication and creating a supportive environment can significantly ease the transition.

Understanding the Impact of Workplace Change

Rohit's experience underscores the reality of working in a rapidly changing environment, especially in industries like tech that thrive on innovation. Change can lead to uncertainty, fear, and resistance among employees, which can negatively impact morale and productivity. Understanding the emotional responses to change is crucial for leaders to effectively manage their teams through transitions.

Rohit's proactive approach to fostering communication and support helped his team cope with the stresses of change. By prioritizing open dialogue and seeking solutions, he created a culture of resilience that allowed the team to thrive even amidst uncertainty.

Strategies for Coping with Change

1. **Embrace a Growth Mindset**
   Rohit began viewing each change as a learning opportunity rather than a disruption. This mindset shift helped him become more open to new experiences.
2. **Focus on What You Can Control**
   Rather than stressing over uncertainties, Rohit concentrated on tasks within his control, such as meeting his own project deadlines and staying organized.

3. **Stay Informed and Ask Questions**
   Rohit made an effort to attend company meetings and ask questions about changes. Staying informed allowed him to adjust faster and understand the rationale behind each decision.

4. **Practice Mindfulness for Emotional Stability**
   Mindfulness exercises helped Rohit remain grounded amid uncertainty. By staying present, he reduced his stress and improved his focus on current tasks.

5. **Seek Support from Peers and Mentors**
   Connecting with colleagues who were also affected by changes provided him with emotional support and practical advice on navigating the shifts.

Reflections and Exercises

- **Reflection Prompt**: List three changes at work that have affected you and how you can reframe them as growth opportunities.

- **Affirmation**: "I am adaptable and resilient in the face of change."

Takeaways from Rohit's Story

1. **Acknowledge the Impact of Change**: Recognize that change can evoke feelings of anxiety and frustration among team members. Validating these emotions is essential to fostering a supportive environment.

2. **Encourage Open Communication**: Create a safe space for team members to express their concerns and challenges. Open dialogue can facilitate understanding and collaboration.

3. **Advocate for Resources**: If changes are poorly managed, don't hesitate to advocate for additional resources such as training or adjusted timelines. Leaders should actively seek solutions that benefit the team.

4. **Foster Team Collaboration**: Encourage collaboration among team members through buddy systems or group projects. This can

help individuals learn from one another and create a sense of camaraderie.

5. **Implement Regular Check-Ins**: Establish regular meetings to monitor progress and address ongoing challenges. These check-ins can foster accountability and celebrate achievements.

6. **Prioritize Self-Care**: Encourage both yourself and your team to practice self-care during times of change. This can help manage stress and maintain a positive outlook.

7. **Embrace Flexibility**: Cultivate a mindset of flexibility and adaptability. Change is a constant in the workplace, and embracing it can lead to growth and innovation.

Rohit's story illustrates that while adapting to change can be challenging, it also presents opportunities for growth and collaboration. By fostering an environment of support and communication, leaders can help their teams thrive in the face of uncertainty, turning challenges into successes.

Chapter 14: Balancing a Side Hustle with Full-Time Work

Story of Sneha: Pursuing a Passion Project Alongside a Corporate Job

Sneha had always been a go-getter. She worked as a financial analyst at a reputable firm, a job she excelled at but didn't find deeply fulfilling. Her real passion lay in art, specifically painting. For years, she'd dreamed of turning her love for painting into a business, but like many, she felt trapped by the security and routine of her corporate job. She wanted the stability of her full-time work but also craved the creative freedom of her art.

After much contemplation, Sneha decided to take the plunge and start a small art business on the side. She would paint custom portraits, landscapes, and abstract pieces in her free time, selling her work online and through social media. Her first few weeks as a side hustler were exhilarating, and she loved the sense of purpose it brought to her life.

However, the reality of juggling a demanding job with her passion project soon hit hard. Late nights and weekends were spent fulfilling orders, managing her social media, and answering customer inquiries. This left her little time to recharge, and she started noticing the effects on her full-time work as well. She was more tired during the day, struggling to concentrate in meetings, and beginning to miss some deadlines. Her performance at work started to slip, and her manager noticed.

Overwhelmed and fearing burnout, Sneha realized she needed a more sustainable way to balance her job and her passion. She decided to seek advice from colleagues and friends who had managed similar dual responsibilities. They suggested setting clear boundaries for her side hustle and establishing a structured schedule to manage her time effectively.

Taking this advice, Sneha blocked out specific hours for her art business, setting boundaries around her availability. She decided that weekday evenings would be devoted to her side hustle, while weekends would be her time for creative work and personal relaxation. She also automated as much of her art business as possible, setting up social media posts in advance and using templates for customer responses.

To help her manage stress, Sneha practiced self-care techniques, including mindfulness meditation and short breaks to recharge. She created a comfortable workspace at home, where she could seamlessly transition between her corporate tasks and her art. Over time, Sneha found a balance that allowed her to excel at her job while nurturing her passion. She learned to be strategic about the hours she put into her art business, focusing on quality over quantity and setting realistic goals for its growth.

With this new approach, Sneha was able to bring her best self to both her roles. Her performance at her marketing job improved, and her art business continued to thrive, bringing in a steady side income. Her passion project was no longer a source of stress but a deeply fulfilling part of her life. Sneha had managed to strike a balance, proving to herself that she could honor her artistic dreams without compromising her career.

Understanding the Challenges of Balancing a Side Hustle

Sneha's journey is one that many professionals face today. In a world where the gig economy and passion projects are becoming increasingly popular, more people are exploring side hustles as an additional income source or as a way to pursue creative interests. However, balancing a full-time career with a side hustle requires careful planning, discipline, and a commitment to self-care. Without a structured approach, the risk of burnout and compromised work performance is high.

Sneha's experience highlights that while having a side hustle is rewarding, it's essential to set clear boundaries and manage time effectively. Success in both areas requires resilience, a proactive mindset, and strategies to ensure both career and passion receive adequate attention without overwhelming the individual.

Strategies for Balancing a Side Hustle and Full-Time Work

1. **Create a Structured Schedule**
   Sneha blocked out specific times for her side hustle, ensuring her work hours didn't interfere with her corporate responsibilities.
2. **Set Boundaries with Clients and Customers**

She established boundaries for her jewelry business, such as specific hours for responding to inquiries, to prevent it from intruding on her primary job.

3. **Prioritize Rest and Self-Care**
   To avoid burnout, Sneha incorporated regular self-care practices and set aside one day a week for rest, without any work.

4. **Automate and Outsource Where Possible**
   Sneha automated certain tasks, such as scheduling social media posts, and outsourced minor tasks like packaging, freeing up time for herself.

5. **Track Progress and Celebrate Milestones**
   By setting small goals for her side hustle, Sneha stayed motivated and celebrated each milestone, making the journey more rewarding.

Reflections and Exercises

- **Journal Exercise**: List three boundaries you can set between your full-time job and your side hustle to maintain balance.

- **Affirmation**: "I am capable of achieving my dreams while maintaining balance and self-care."

Takeaways from Sneha's Story

1. **Establish Boundaries and Structure**: Clearly define when and how much time you'll devote to your side hustle to avoid burnout. Having a structured schedule helps in managing both roles without compromising on either.

2. **Prioritize Self-Care**: Managing a full-time job and a side hustle can be demanding, so regular self-care is essential. Practice mindfulness, exercise, or other activities that recharge you mentally and physically.

3. **Use Automation and Efficiency Tools**: Leveraging technology for tasks like scheduling social media posts or automating customer responses can save time and reduce stress. Find ways to simplify repetitive tasks.

4. **Set Realistic Goals for Your Side Hustle**: Growing a side business takes time. Focus on manageable, incremental growth rather than expecting quick success, which can lead to exhaustion and frustration.

5. **Seek Support from Colleagues and Friends**: Discussing your dual responsibilities with people who've been in similar situations can offer valuable insights. Their advice and encouragement can make balancing multiple roles more achievable.

6. **Learn to Transition Smoothly Between Roles**: Creating a dedicated workspace and having a specific time for each role helps the mind switch between tasks efficiently, reducing the cognitive strain of frequent shifts.

7. **Regularly Evaluate Your Goals:** Check in with yourself to assess whether your side hustle is adding to your life or becoming a burden. Adjust your approach as needed to ensure it remains fulfilling and sustainable.

Sneha's story is a testament to the power of balance, dedication, and boundaries. By honoring both her career and her creative passion, she was able to find personal fulfillment and professional success. Her journey serves as a guide for anyone looking to pursue their dreams without compromising their career stability.

Chapter 15: Surviving Long Work Hours and Overtime

Story of Ajay: A Consultant's Struggle with Exhaustion

Ajay was the epitome of ambition. Working as a consultant for one of the top firms in the industry, he was known for his analytical skills, client-centered approach, and commitment to excellence. He thrived on the challenge of each project, often working across multiple time zones, spending hours in airports, and attending back-to-back meetings. But as his responsibilities grew, so did the pressure. While his dedication had initially earned him praise and promotions, it eventually began to erode his energy and enthusiasm.

Initially, Ajay believed he could push through it. Long hours, disrupted sleep, and constant travel were simply part of the job, he thought. However, over time, he found himself feeling exhausted even after a good night's rest. His productivity declined, and he struggled to focus during meetings. He became irritable, lost patience with colleagues, and felt disconnected from the work that once excited him.

As the pressure mounted, Ajay felt trapped. He knew he was struggling, but he felt he couldn't show vulnerability in such a competitive environment. His family began to notice the toll his job was taking on him; he was often absent at family gatherings, and when he was present, he was too drained to engage. His physical health suffered too, with constant migraines, sinusitis and a sense of fatigue that even a weekend off couldn't cure.

One evening, after missing an important family event due to last-minute work changes, Ajay hit his breaking point. The guilt of letting down his loved ones coupled with his mounting frustration at work pushed him to reflect on his life choices. He realized that he couldn't continue down this path without sacrificing his health and happiness. Ajay confided in a close friend and mentor, who recommended he seek guidance from a wellness coach experienced in managing workplace stress and burnout.

Through counseling, Ajay learned about the phenomenon of burnout, especially in high-stakes consulting roles. He realized that he'd placed an unrelenting burden on himself to succeed, often at the expense of his well-being. Together with his counselor, Ajay developed strategies for setting boundaries, managing stress, and regaining control over his schedule. He also started incorporating small wellness practices, such as taking breaks throughout the day and ensuring he disconnected from work in the evenings.

Over time, Ajay began to see a significant shift. He learned to delegate more and set limits on his working hours. He took regular breaks, returned to his hobbies, and made a conscious effort to be present for his family. With these adjustments, Ajay found himself approaching his work with renewed energy and clarity, regaining the enthusiasm he had when he first entered the field.

Understanding the Impact of Long Work Hours

Long work hours are often seen as a hallmark of dedication and drive in today's professional world. Yet, as work demands increase, there's a growing need to examine the real effects that extended hours have on employees. While working late or taking on additional tasks may boost productivity temporarily, the cumulative impact on mental, physical, and emotional health can be significant.

Extended hours often lead to chronic stress, fatigue, and burnout. Physically, long hours can result in sleep deprivation, increased risk of cardiovascular issues, and weakened immune response. Mentally, it can lead to reduced cognitive function, lower creativity, and decreased problem-solving skills. Emotional exhaustion often follows, impacting mood, reducing patience, and making it challenging to maintain positive relationships with coworkers and loved ones.

The psychological toll of constantly working overtime is also substantial. Professionals may feel a constant sense of guilt or inadequacy, worrying that they haven't done "enough" regardless of their actual accomplishments. This can create a vicious cycle, where the stress of trying to meet expectations leads to even longer hours, eventually resulting in burnout.

In today's competitive work culture, it's essential for both employers and employees to understand the importance of work-life balance. Studies show that while long hours may bring temporary gains, sustainable productivity requires regular breaks, reasonable workloads, and respect for personal time. By encouraging a healthier balance, companies can reduce employee turnover, increase job satisfaction, and foster a more innovative and motivated workforce.

Strategies for Managing Long Work Hours and Preventing Burnout

1. Prioritize and Delegate Tasks

Ajay took a closer look at his workload and identified tasks that could either be delegated to team members or completed later. He started each day by making a list of the most critical tasks and focusing on completing those during his peak productivity hours. Delegating smaller tasks allowed him to reserve his energy for high-priority projects, reducing the number of late nights.

2. Communicate Boundaries Clearly

Ajay recognized the need to communicate his limits with his manager and team. By discussing his workload and potential effects on his performance, he could express his commitment to quality rather than just hours worked. He arranged weekly check-ins with his manager to ensure they shared the same priorities, which made it easier to set realistic deadlines. Establishing these boundaries also gave him permission to end his workday at a reasonable hour.

3. Incorporate Small Breaks and Practice the 90-Minute Rule

To avoid complete mental exhaustion, Ajay adopted the 90-minute rule, working in focused intervals with short breaks in between. By breaking his day into manageable segments, he felt less drained and was able to maintain his focus longer. He used breaks to stretch, grab a coffee, or simply take a few deep breaths, which recharged his energy and allowed him to return to his tasks with a refreshed mind.

4. Advocate for a Manageable Workload

During his performance reviews, Ajay raised the issue of excessive overtime, focusing on how it was affecting his productivity and mental well-being. He approached this conversation diplomatically, emphasizing his desire to continue delivering quality work but within a sustainable framework. His supervisor recognized his commitment and agreed to bring in an additional team member, allowing the workload to be more evenly distributed.

5. Schedule Time for Rest and Recovery

Ajay began scheduling personal time just as he would any important work meeting. He set aside weekends for family activities and personal pursuits, and during the week, he dedicated evenings to unwinding. This scheduled time for rest helped him regain his energy and maintain a healthier work-life balance. Knowing he had these breaks to look forward to made it easier for him to concentrate during work hours.

6. Set Realistic Goals and Be Open to Saying No

Rather than trying to complete every project or please every client, Ajay set realistic expectations for himself and learned the power of saying no. He evaluated each new task's priority level and only committed to projects that were aligned with his professional goals. By politely declining non-urgent tasks, he could focus on essential responsibilities without spreading himself too thin.

Reflections and Exercises

- **Reflection Prompt**: Think of a time when you felt overburdened by work. What strategies did you use to cope, and what could you have done differently?

- **Journal Exercise**: Make a list of three work-related tasks you could either delegate, delay, or simplify. Consider implementing one change to lighten your workload this week.

- **Affirmation**: "I am dedicated to my work, but I also honor my need for rest and balance. I can achieve my goals while maintaining my well-being."

Takeaways from Ajay's Story

1. **Recognize and Address Burnout Early**: Burnout isn't just prolonged fatigue; it's a serious state of physical, emotional, and mental exhaustion. Recognizing the early signs allows for timely intervention, potentially preventing deeper issues.

2. **Set Boundaries and Delegate**: In high-pressure environments, setting boundaries around work hours and learning to delegate are key. This allows you to manage workload effectively and prevents overextension.

3. **Practice Consistent Self-Care**: Prioritize activities that recharge you. Whether it's hobbies, spending time with family, or regular exercise, self-care helps restore energy and resilience.

4. **Value Connection Outside of Work**: Reconnecting with loved ones and making time for personal life contributes to a balanced life. These relationships provide support and perspective outside of work's demands.

5. **Seek Support When Needed**: There's no shame in seeking professional help to navigate burnout. Career counselors or wellness coaches can offer valuable tools to create a healthier balance.

6. **Reevaluate Your Long-Term Goals**: Regularly assessing whether your current career path aligns with your values and lifestyle is crucial. For Ajay, shifting focus from endless deadlines to sustainable work allowed him to continue excelling without compromising his well-being.

7. **Focus on What Brings Joy in Work**: Over time, it's easy to lose sight of what you love in a demanding role. Reconnecting with your initial passion can bring purpose and perspective back into your career.

   Ajay's story highlights that achieving success doesn't have to come at the cost of personal well-being. Setting boundaries, maintaining personal connections, and consistently practicing self-care can prevent burnout and allow for a fulfilling career.

Chapter 16: Handling Interpersonal Conflicts

Story of Tanya: Conflict with a Teammate

Tanya was a driven, detail-oriented marketing professional known for her high standards and strong work ethic. She thrived in her role, but when she was paired with another marketing manager, Ravi, on a major project, things took an unexpected turn. While Tanya liked structure and a methodical approach, Ravi was more spontaneous and believed in improvisation. Their differing styles led to a series of misunderstandings and escalating tensions as they tried to collaborate on the project.

From the beginning, Tanya felt frustrated by Ravi's approach. She often found him missing agreed-upon deadlines, which made her feel that her hard work was being undermined. Meanwhile, Ravi found Tanya's attention to detail and insistence on rigid timelines constraining, feeling she was too controlling and inflexible. Their differing styles quickly evolved from minor disagreements to open frustration, and soon their conflicts started to affect the entire team's morale.

The tension came to a head during a team meeting, where Tanya and Ravi's argument became so heated that the meeting had to be paused. Afterward, their manager intervened, urging both of them to have a private conversation to clear the air. Reluctantly, Tanya agreed, and she and Ravi met with a mediator to discuss their issues.

During their conversation, Tanya learned that Ravi hadn't been ignoring deadlines out of disrespect but rather had been struggling to juggle multiple projects without letting anyone know he was overwhelmed. In turn, Ravi came to understand that Tanya's insistence on deadlines stemmed from her desire to keep the team's work organized and effective. They both realized that their assumptions about each other's intentions were incorrect, and this misunderstanding had fueled their frustrations.

With the help of the mediator, they worked on creating a balance between Tanya's structured approach and Ravi's adaptability. They agreed to set check-in points throughout the project and keep open lines of communication. They also set some clear boundaries and decided on shared responsibilities to respect each other's strengths.

As their project continued, both Tanya and Ravi found their dynamic had significantly improved. Tanya felt less frustrated and more at ease with flexibility, while Ravi began to appreciate the value of planning. Their shared success on the project also helped to rebuild their professional relationship, and they each gained a new respect for one another's unique approach.

Understanding the Nature of Interpersonal Conflict

Conflict with a teammate is common in professional settings, especially when personalities and work styles clash. While it can be challenging to work with someone whose methods differ significantly from one's own, these experiences offer valuable learning opportunities. Miscommunication often sits at the heart of most workplace conflicts. When people assume negative intentions or focus solely on differences, it becomes difficult to see the value in the other person's approach.

It's also common for people to view their own perspective as the "right" one, without considering that their teammate's approach may be valid in its own way. By approaching these conflicts with curiosity and a willingness to understand the other person's motivations, employees can turn tense situations into collaborative growth opportunities. As with Tanya and Ravi, addressing the conflict openly and with the support of a neutral third party, if necessary, can help bridge differences, rebuild respect, and foster a more cooperative working environment.

Strategies to overcome Interpersonal Conflict

1. **Understand Different Perspectives**

    Tanya recognized that understanding Amit's approach could help alleviate tensions. She initiated a conversation to discuss their differing work styles, aiming to find common ground. By expressing genuine interest in his perspective, she learned that Amit thrived under pressure and often produced his best work last minute.

2. **Communicate Openly**

    Clear communication became Tanya's priority. Rather than making assumptions about Amit's intentions, she learned to express her concerns directly. During a team meeting, she framed her thoughts using "I" statements, saying, "I feel stressed when deadlines are tight, and I worry about our project's success."

3. **Set Boundaries and Expectations**

Together, they worked on setting clear expectations for the project. Tanya proposed regular check-ins to monitor progress, which allowed Amit to share updates on his tasks without last-minute surprises. This structure provided Tanya with a sense of control while respecting Amit's work style.

4. **Seek Mediation**

When tensions remained high, Tanya suggested involving their supervisor for mediation. This neutral perspective helped clarify misunderstandings and allowed both parties to voice their concerns in a constructive environment.

5. **Focus on Team Goals**

By redirecting their focus to the project's collective goals, Tanya and Amit learned to collaborate more effectively. They established a shared vision, reminding themselves that they were working towards a common objective, which helped to reduce personal conflicts.

Reflections and Exercises

- **Reflection Prompt**: Think of a recent conflict you experienced at work. What were the underlying issues, and how could open communication have changed the outcome?

- **Journal Exercise**: Write down three strategies you can use to approach interpersonal conflicts more constructively in the future.

- **Affirmation**: "I approach conflicts with an open mind and a willingness to understand others. I value collaboration and seek solutions that benefit everyone involved."

Takeaway from Tanya's Story

1. **Open Communication is Key**: Instead of allowing misunderstandings to fester, addressing issues directly and with empathy can prevent escalation.

2. **Assume Positive Intent**: Often, workplace conflicts are fueled by misinterpretations. Assuming positive intent can help you see situations more objectively.

3. **Value Different Perspectives**: Diverse work styles can complement each other, leading to more comprehensive and creative solutions when appreciated.

4. **Seek Mediation if Needed**: In situations where conflicts become intense, seeking the support of a manager, HR, or mediator can help facilitate productive conversations and rebuild professional relationships.

5. **Focus on Collaboration, Not Competition**: By focusing on shared goals and valuing each team member's contribution, conflicts can be turned into opportunities for personal growth and team cohesion.

Tanya's experience with Ravi illustrates that while team conflicts are uncomfortable, they're also normal and can be resolved. Approaching conflict with openness, empathy, and a willingness to adapt allows individuals and teams to thrive even in challenging situations.

Chapter 17: Navigating Workplace Discrimination

Story of Farah: Facing Subtle Bias

Farah had been a dedicated employee at her consulting firm for several years, known for her analytical skills and strategic thinking. Despite her qualifications and consistent performance, Farah began to notice small, unsettling behaviors from some colleagues and superiors that left her feeling isolated. She felt her ideas were often overlooked in meetings until they were echoed by others, and she frequently received vague feedback compared to her peers, who got more constructive guidance. Farah also noticed that she wasn't given certain high-visibility projects, despite her interest and qualifications.

Initially, Farah questioned if she was being overly sensitive. After all, nothing her colleagues said or did was overtly discriminatory. However, as the pattern continued, she couldn't ignore the nagging feeling of being treated differently. She felt marginalized, yet unsure how to address her concerns since they were based on subtle actions and unspoken attitudes rather than explicit statements.

Feeling frustrated, Farah decided to talk to a trusted colleague, Maya, who had a similar experience. Maya encouraged Farah to observe patterns and keep track of specific instances that made her feel sidelined. With Maya's advice, Farah began noting down instances, such as when she was overlooked for projects, when her ideas were dismissed or repeated by others, and when feedback was given in a way that felt less helpful than it should be.

Armed with examples, Farah finally decided to have a private conversation with her supervisor. During their meeting, she calmly explained her feelings and presented the observations she had recorded. She expressed her commitment to her role and desire for more inclusive feedback and opportunities for advancement. Her supervisor was initially taken aback but listened attentively. He acknowledged that unconscious biases could sometimes shape workplace interactions and thanked Farah for bringing these issues to his attention.

Over the next few months, Farah noticed changes. She was assigned to projects more aligned with her skill set and began receiving more constructive feedback. Her colleagues started including her more in discussions, and her ideas were taken more seriously. Though it was a gradual shift, Farah felt empowered by the steps she took to address her concerns and was proud that her firm had responded positively.

Understanding Workplace Discrimination

Subtle bias, also known as microaggressions, can be challenging to identify and address because it often manifests in indirect ways. Unlike overt discrimination, subtle bias tends to be expressed through actions, body language, or choices that can feel dismissive, minimizing, or exclusionary. These behaviors can impact an individual's confidence, sense of belonging, and even career growth, creating an invisible barrier that can be difficult to break through.

Subtle bias often stems from unconscious beliefs or stereotypes that shape how people perceive and interact with others. Those who experience it may feel like they're overreacting or misinterpreting interactions, which can prevent them from speaking up. However, over time, such biases can lead to frustration, decreased morale, and a lack of trust in the workplace.

It's important to recognize that subtle bias can impact both individuals and organizations, affecting team cohesion and productivity. Addressing these biases requires openness to feedback, self-awareness, and a commitment to fostering an inclusive and respectful environment.

Strategies for Navigating Workplace Discrimination

1. **Document Experiences**

   Farah began keeping a detailed record of incidents, noting the context and responses of her colleagues. This documentation provided her with clarity and validation, helping her understand the patterns of behavior she faced.

2. **Seek Allies and Mentors**

   Realizing she wasn't alone; Farah reached out to supportive colleagues and found a mentor within the company. This network offered her guidance and a sense of belonging, reinforcing her confidence in navigating her workplace challenges.

3. **Communicate Assertively**

Farah learned to assert herself in meetings by ensuring her contributions were acknowledged. She made it a point to follow up on her ideas, providing additional context and seeking feedback. This proactive approach gradually increased her visibility and credibility among her peers.

4. **Utilize HR Resources**

    Armed with her documentation, Farah approached HR to discuss her experiences. They provided her with resources on the company's diversity and inclusion policies, empowering her to advocate for herself and others.

5. **Engage in Diversity Initiatives**

    Farah volunteered for company diversity initiatives, which helped raise awareness of discrimination issues. By participating in workshops and discussions, she not only educated herself but also contributed to a broader dialogue within the organization.

Reflections and Exercises

-   **Reflection Prompt**: Have you experienced or witnessed discrimination at work? What steps did you take, or could you have taken, to address the situation?

-   **Journal Exercise**: Identify three allies in your workplace who can support you in creating a more inclusive environment.

-   **Affirmation**: "I stand firm in my value and contributions. I am deserving of respect and recognition, and I actively contribute to a diverse and inclusive workplace."

Takeaway from Farah's Story

1. **Trust Your Instincts:** If you feel marginalized or dismissed, trust that feeling rather than second-guessing yourself. Subtle biases are often difficult to recognize but are real and can impact your well-being.

2. **Document Patterns**: Keep track of specific examples of bias. This documentation can help you clearly communicate your concerns if you decide to address them with others.

3. **Seek Support**: Talking to a trusted colleague or mentor can provide perspective and support, especially if they have faced similar situations. Allies in the workplace can validate your experiences and offer guidance.

4. **Address Concerns Calmly and Professionally**: If you choose to bring up your concerns, approach it in a constructive manner. Present specific examples and focus on your commitment to your role and growth within the organization.

5. **Encourage Organizational Change:** Organizations benefit from acknowledging subtle biases and working towards a more inclusive environment. Open feedback mechanisms can help create an atmosphere where all employees feel valued and respected.

Farah's experience highlights the challenges and impact of subtle bias. By trusting her instincts and advocating for herself professionally, she was able to initiate positive change in her workplace. Her story serves as a reminder that addressing even subtle forms of discrimination is essential for fostering an inclusive and supportive work environment.

Chapter 18: Managing Self-Doubt After Failure

Story of Vikas: Overcoming the Stigma of a Project Failure

Vikas was an ambitious project manager who always went above and beyond to ensure his projects met the highest standards. Recently, he was handed a high-stakes project for a top client—a project that, if successful, could open up new opportunities for his team and enhance his professional reputation. He poured all his energy into it, working long hours, coordinating with cross-functional teams, and meticulously checking every detail.

But things didn't go as planned. A critical vendor failed to deliver on time, and unexpected technical issues arose during the final stages. Despite Vikas's best efforts, the project was delayed and fell short of client expectations. The client was unhappy, and Vikas's team faced scrutiny from upper management. Vikas was devastated; he felt the weight of the failure personally and started doubting his abilities. Although he knew some factors were beyond his control, he couldn't shake off the feeling that he had let everyone down.

Vikas soon noticed a shift in how his colleagues and superiors treated him. Team members who once sought his advice began avoiding his input, and management seemed more cautious about assigning him new responsibilities. Even socially, he felt people were looking at him differently. Vikas felt as though his failure had branded him as incapable, and the stigma made it hard for him to move forward. He became anxious and struggled with self-doubt, wondering if he'd ever regain his reputation.

After a few difficult weeks, Vikas decided he needed to confront this head-on. He reached out to his mentor, a senior leader who had navigated a similar setback in his own career. His mentor encouraged him to analyze the project objectively and identify both the external challenges and areas where he could have improved. This exercise allowed Vikas to see the situation more clearly, helping him realize that while he had made some mistakes, much of the failure was due to factors beyond his control.

With this perspective, Vikas decided to reframe his narrative. He presented a lessons-learned report to his manager, highlighting not only the challenges faced but also the improvements he'd implement in future projects. He also requested more training in risk management, showing his commitment to growth and resilience. Gradually, management noticed his proactive attitude, and he was assigned to another project—albeit a smaller one initially. Vikas approached this new project with a renewed focus and eventually succeeded, regaining the trust of his team and supervisors.

In time, Vikas learned to embrace his past mistake as a learning experience rather than a permanent mark on his career. He understood that resilience and adaptability were just as important as success in building a solid reputation.

Understanding Self-Doubt and Its Impact

Failure is a part of every career, but in many workplaces, the stigma surrounding it can be intense. Individuals who experience failure may feel that it defines them, often leading to feelings of shame, self-doubt, and anxiety. This stigma can hinder an employee's growth and morale, especially when colleagues or superiors reinforce it, either intentionally or unintentionally.

Workplace culture often dictates how failure is perceived. In supportive environments, failure is seen as an opportunity to learn and improve. However, in more rigid or high-stakes environments, it can feel like a permanent blemish. The reality is that failure is frequently a result of multiple factors, including those beyond an individual's control, and reframing it constructively is crucial to moving forward.

Strategies for Managing Self-Doubt After Failure

1. **Reframe Failure as a Learning Opportunity**

   Vikas began to see failure as a stepping stone rather than an endpoint. He acknowledged that mistakes provided valuable lessons and opportunities for growth. This shift in perspective allowed him to approach future projects with a more open mind.

2. **Seek Constructive Feedback**

   Instead of avoiding conversations about the failed project, Vikas sought feedback from his manager and peers. He asked specific questions to understand what went wrong and how he could improve. This constructive criticism helped him identify actionable steps for future success.

3. **Practice Self-Compassion**

Vikas learned the importance of being kind to himself. He started practicing self-compassion by reminding himself that everyone makes mistakes and that one failure does not define his entire career. Journaling about his feelings helped him process his emotions and foster self-acceptance.

4. **Set Small, Achievable Goals**

To rebuild his confidence, Vikas set small, realistic goals for himself. Completing these tasks successfully reinforced his capabilities and gradually restored his self-esteem. Each success served as a reminder that he was still competent and capable of growth.

5. **Embrace a Growth Mindset**

Vikas adopted a growth mindset, viewing challenges as opportunities for development. He began to embrace risks, understanding that discomfort often leads to personal and professional advancement.

Reflections and Exercises

- **Reflection Prompt**: Think of a time when you faced failure. How did it affect your confidence, and what did you learn from the experience?

- **Journal Exercise**: List three lessons you've learned from past failures and how they have contributed to your growth.

- **Affirmation**: "I acknowledge my mistakes as part of my journey. I am resilient, and each setback only makes me stronger and more capable."

Takeaway from Vikas's Story

1. **Seek Objectivity**: When dealing with a setback, try to objectively analyze the factors that led to it. Separate elements that were within your control from those that weren't. This can help reduce self-blame and encourage a balanced view of the situation.

2. **Embrace a Growth Mindset**: Look at failure as a learning experience. Use it to identify areas where you can grow, whether it's through additional training, seeking mentorship, or building new skills.

3. **Communicate Transparently:** Proactively share what you've learned with your manager or team. Presenting solutions and a plan for improvement demonstrates maturity and accountability, showing others that you are committed to growth.

4. **Redefine Success**: Remember that success isn't only about delivering results; it's also about resilience, adaptability, and the ability to navigate challenges. Bouncing back from failure is often a more powerful testament to your abilities than success alone.

5. **Move Forward Confidently**: Once you've learned from the experience, don't let the failure define you. Take on new projects with the same passion and confidence, using your previous experience to handle challenges more effectively.

Vikas's journey shows that setbacks don't have to be career-ending. By facing his mistake, learning from it, and reframing it as a growth opportunity, Vikas demonstrated resilience and regained his professional standing. His story is a powerful reminder that failures are stepping stones to growth, and facing them with courage can open new doors.

Chapter 19: Adapting to a New Role or Promotion

Story of Aditi: Adjusting to Leadership

Aditi had been a dedicated and high-performing team member in her organization for years. Her attention to detail, commitment, and reliability didn't go unnoticed; when a leadership position opened up, her superiors quickly promoted her to manage the team. It was a role she had dreamed of, and she was thrilled at the chance to contribute to her company's success in a new way. But as the reality of her new responsibilities set in, Aditi felt both excitement and a deep sense of unease.

In her new role, Aditi quickly realized that her responsibilities weren't just about executing tasks, but about guiding a team, making strategic decisions, and representing the interests of both her team members and the company. Her first major challenge came when her team missed a critical deadline on a high-profile project. Despite her best efforts to motivate her team, they had encountered unforeseen challenges. Aditi found herself juggling the disappointment of upper management and the low morale of her team. For the first time, she experienced feelings of isolation and self-doubt; she questioned her own leadership skills and felt that she had let everyone down.

As the pressure mounted, Aditi struggled with finding her own leadership style. She initially tried to emulate her previous boss, someone she had admired greatly, but found that their assertive and authoritative approach didn't come naturally to her. Her attempts to be a strict manager felt forced, and her team began to notice the change. They felt Aditi was becoming distant, and communication issues started to arise. What was once a friendly, collaborative work environment turned tense and uneasy.

In search of clarity, Aditi reached out to a mentor within the organization—a senior leader known for his empathetic and approachable leadership style. Through their conversations, her mentor helped her understand that effective leadership doesn't mean embodying someone else's traits but finding a style that aligns with her own strengths and values. Aditi recognized that she was naturally more collaborative and preferred open communication, empathy, and trust-building within her team. Embracing these qualities, she started holding one-on-one sessions with her team members, actively listening to their feedback, and making adjustments where necessary.

Gradually, Aditi found that as she embraced her authentic self, her team responded positively. They began to trust her and felt comfortable bringing up challenges, allowing her to address issues early on. Aditi focused on creating a supportive environment that encouraged growth and innovation, where team members felt safe sharing ideas without fear of judgment. She realized that leadership wasn't about being perfect or rigidly following a specific model; it was about supporting her team, enabling them to do their best work, and being adaptable.

Over time, Aditi grew more confident in her role. She learned to balance the demands of upper management with the needs of her team, and the culture of openness and trust she fostered led to improved productivity and morale. She embraced the idea that her role as a leader was as much about serving her team as it was about achieving results. This shift not only transformed her leadership style but also created a ripple effect, inspiring others in her team to take ownership of their roles and approach their work with renewed enthusiasm.

Understanding the Challenges of New Roles

Transitioning from an individual contributor to a leadership position can be a complex and often challenging experience. New leaders may find themselves struggling with self-doubt, imposter syndrome, and the pressure to live up to expectations. Unlike task-oriented roles, leadership requires balancing team dynamics, managing conflicts, making strategic decisions, and representing the interests of both the team and the organization. Often, first-time leaders feel they need to emulate someone else's style, even if it doesn't suit them.

True leadership emerges when individuals find their authentic style, leveraging their natural strengths to build trust and motivate their teams. Being a successful leader is not about perfection; it's about being adaptable, empathetic, and fostering a supportive environment where team members can thrive. Recognizing that leadership is a journey of self-discovery and growth is essential for making the transition smoother and more fulfilling.

Strategies for Adapting to a New Role or Promotion

    1. **Build Leadership Skills**

Aditi enrolled in leadership training to enhance her skills. She focused on effective communication, decision-making, and team management. This training provided her with practical tools and boosted her confidence in her new position.

2. **Seek Mentorship**

Finding a mentor within the organization who had successfully navigated a similar transition proved invaluable. Her mentor provided insights, shared experiences, and offered advice on handling challenges specific to her new role.

3. **Embrace Vulnerability**
Aditi learned to embrace vulnerability by openly discussing her uncertainties with her team. By sharing her feelings, she created a culture of trust and encouraged her team members to voice their concerns, fostering an environment of open communication.

4. **Set Realistic Expectations**

Aditi understood that it was essential to set realistic expectations for herself and her team. She established clear, achievable goals, which helped her focus on progress rather than perfection.

5. **Celebrate Small Wins**

Recognizing and celebrating small accomplishments helped Aditi build momentum. By acknowledging her team's efforts and her own progress, she fostered a positive work environment and boosted morale.

Reflections and Exercises

- **Reflection Prompt**: Reflect on a time when you faced a significant transition in your career. What challenges did you encounter, and how did you overcome them?

- **Journal Exercise**: List three qualities you bring to your new role that make you a valuable leader.

- **Affirmation**: "I embrace my new role with confidence and openness. I am a capable leader, and I grow stronger with each challenge I face."

Takeaways from Aditi's Story

1. **Find Your Authentic Leadership Style**: Embrace the qualities that make you unique rather than trying to mimic someone else's style. Authenticity fosters trust and respect within your team and enables you to lead with confidence.

2. **Prioritize Open Communication**: Regular check-ins and open communication with team members can help uncover potential issues early and foster a positive work environment where feedback is valued.

3. **Balance Task and People Management**: A successful leader balances the needs of the organization with those of the team. While results are essential, it's also important to be approachable and empathetic, creating an environment where people feel motivated and supported.

4. **Be Adaptable and Learn from Mistakes**: Adjusting to a leadership role is a continuous process. Mistakes and setbacks are inevitable; use them as learning opportunities rather than signs of failure.

5. **Embrace a Growth Mindset**: Leadership is a journey, not a destination. Embrace the growth and challenges that come with the role, and be open to learning and evolving.

Aditi's journey highlights that leadership is not about rigidly following a prescribed set of rules or embodying another's traits. Instead, it's about finding what feels natural, building trust, and focusing on the collective growth of the team. Her story reminds new leaders that it's okay to make mistakes as they find their footing, and that genuine connection and understanding are often the most powerful tools in a leader's toolkit.

Chapter 20: Planning for a Career Change

Story of Deepak: Contemplating a Major Shift

Deepak had built a stable, successful career as a senior manager at a multinational corporation, a role he had been in for nearly a decade. His work was well-respected, he was well-compensated, and he enjoyed a degree of influence and autonomy within the organization. However, despite the outward signs of success, Deepak felt increasingly unfulfilled. Over the years, his passion for his work had waned, and he found himself questioning the purpose of his daily routine. The corporate culture he once enjoyed now felt monotonous, and he wondered if his skills and energy might be better applied elsewhere.

As these feelings persisted, Deepak began to contemplate a major shift in his life: the possibility of leaving his corporate career to pursue something more meaningful and aligned with his values. He felt drawn to work in the social sector, where he believed his managerial skills could make a positive impact. However, the idea of leaving the financial stability, familiarity, and security of his corporate role filled him with doubt and anxiety. He worried about the financial repercussions, the reaction of his family and friends, and the possibility of regretting his decision if things didn't work out.

One evening, Deepak attended a career transition seminar where he met others who had left high-paying jobs to pursue passion projects or socially impactful work. Listening to their stories of courage, growth, and fulfillment gave him a fresh perspective. Inspired, he decided to begin by volunteering at a local NGO on weekends, to get a feel for the work and determine if he truly connected with it. This experience was transformative; he found himself energized, excited, and deeply satisfied. He felt a sense of purpose he hadn't experienced in years.

The volunteer work confirmed for Deepak that he wanted to make the shift. However, he knew he needed to approach it carefully. He began setting aside savings and preparing a budget to sustain him through the transition period. He also enrolled in online courses related to non-profit management and social entrepreneurship to build skills specific to the sector he wanted to enter. Gradually, Deepak started having conversations with his family, sharing his thoughts and getting their support. He reached out to people in his network who had made similar shifts, learning about both the rewards and the challenges.

After a year of preparation, Deepak finally felt ready to take the leap. He submitted his resignation and began a full-time role with a non-profit focused on education for underprivileged children. The transition wasn't easy—he faced a steep learning curve, and the financial rewards were modest compared to his previous role. However, he found a renewed sense of purpose and fulfillment, knowing his work was making a direct impact on lives.

Looking back, Deepak realized that the fear of change had kept him in his comfort zone for too long. While the corporate world had been a valuable part of his life, his new path was enriching him in ways he had never anticipated. The journey had taught him that change, while daunting, often leads to growth and fulfillment when pursued with passion and purpose.

Understanding the Dynamics of Career Change

Contemplating a major career shift is a deeply personal and often challenging experience. Many individuals, like Deepak, find themselves at a crossroads where they question the purpose and fulfillment of their current roles. This shift in perspective can be spurred by various factors, such as a desire for greater meaning, personal values, or a need for change after years in a stable career. However, the fear of uncertainty, financial instability, and societal expectations often hold people back from pursuing their passions.

Making a successful transition requires a blend of introspection, preparation, and courage. It's essential to take practical steps, such as testing the waters through volunteering, saving a financial buffer, and acquiring relevant skills before making the leap. A gradual, well-planned transition can help individuals build the confidence and security needed to move forward. Ultimately, taking a leap toward meaningful work involves trusting oneself, embracing growth, and remaining adaptable.

Strategies for Planning a Career Change

1. **Assess Transferable Skills**

Deepak took the time to identify the skills he had developed in sales that could be valuable in environmental conservation, such as communication, negotiation, and project management. Recognizing these transferable skills empowered him to see how his background could contribute to his desired field.

2. **Network with Industry Professionals**

Deepak reached out to individuals working in environmental conservation to gain insights into the field. He attended networking events and joined online communities, which helped him understand the industry better and establish valuable connections.

3. **Plan Financially**

Understanding that a career change might involve an initial financial sacrifice, Deepak started a savings plan. He set aside money to cover expenses while he pursued education or training in his new field. This proactive approach alleviated some of his financial fears.

4. **Educate Yourself**

Deepak enrolled in online courses related to environmental science and conservation, equipping himself with relevant knowledge and skills. He also sought volunteer opportunities to gain hands-on experience, enhancing his resume and confidence.

5. **Set a Timeline with Milestones**

Deepak created a realistic plan with specific milestones for his career transition. By breaking down the process into manageable steps, he felt less overwhelmed and could track his progress, celebrating small victories along the way.

Reflections and Exercises

- **Reflection Prompt**: Consider a career change you've contemplated. What fears or uncertainties hold you back, and how can you address them?

- **Journal Exercise**: Outline your career change plan, including the skills you need to develop and the steps you will take to transition successfully.

- **Affirmation**: "I am capable of creating the career I desire. I embrace change with courage and resilience, knowing that my journey leads to fulfillment."

Takeaways from Deepak's Story

1. **Start with Small Steps**: Major changes don't need to happen overnight. Volunteering or taking on small projects related to a new field can help you test your interest and readiness for a full transition.

2. **Plan Financially for the Transition**: A major career shift can come with financial uncertainty, so it's wise to save and prepare a budget that supports you through the transition.

3. **Gain Relevant Skills**: Enrolling in courses or training related to your new field can help you feel better prepared and bridge any skill gaps.

4. **Seek Support and Build Networks**: Talking to others who have made similar transitions can provide valuable insights and emotional support.

5. **Embrace Uncertainty as Part of Growth**: Change can be daunting, but it's often through uncertainty that we find new opportunities, personal growth, and deeper fulfillment.

Deepak's story reminds us that major shifts require both courage and careful planning. For those willing to take the leap, the rewards can be profound, offering renewed purpose and the satisfaction of aligning one's work with one's values.

Chapter 21: Dealing with Performance Pressure and Unrealistic Expectations

Story of Ravi: The Overburdened Employee

Ravi had always been known as a hardworking and dedicated employee in his role as a mid-level project manager. With his positive attitude and commitment to excellence, he was a favorite among both his managers and his peers. However, Ravi's dedication to his job became a double-edged sword as he began to take on more and more responsibilities. His supervisor recognized his reliability and started delegating extra projects to him. As word spread about his work ethic, he found himself at the center of multiple high-stakes projects, each with tight deadlines.

Initially, Ravi felt a sense of pride in handling these tasks. He believed that all his hard work would eventually be recognized with a promotion or raise. But as the months went on, he started feeling physically and emotionally drained. His days stretched long, from early mornings to late evenings, and even weekends became fair game for completing tasks. His personal life was practically non-existent; family gatherings, social events, and hobbies had all fallen to the wayside. Friends and family began to worry, noticing his irritability and fatigue.

Ravi knew something had to change when he experienced a panic attack in the middle of a workday after an intense meeting. This was a turning point, forcing him to acknowledge that his workload had taken a severe toll on his health and well-being. His sleep was restless, his mental health was deteriorating, and his productivity, ironically, was beginning to suffer despite all the extra hours he put in.

Realizing he couldn't continue on this path, Ravi decided to seek advice from a trusted mentor in the company. His mentor, who had experienced similar struggles early in his own career, shared his insights on setting boundaries, communicating effectively, and prioritizing tasks. He advised Ravi to talk to his supervisor and be transparent about his workload. Though initially uncomfortable with the idea, Ravi recognized the need to set boundaries if he wanted to protect his health and sustain his career in the long run.

With a bit of encouragement, Ravi scheduled a meeting with his supervisor and explained his situation honestly. He expressed his willingness to continue giving his best, but he emphasized that he needed a more manageable workload to maintain quality and efficiency. To his surprise, his supervisor responded positively, acknowledging the oversight and expressing appreciation for his candor. Together, they worked out a plan to delegate some of his responsibilities and set realistic deadlines for ongoing projects.

Over time, Ravi learned to balance his commitment to work with the need for self-care. He became more assertive in prioritizing his tasks and comfortable in saying "no" when he felt overwhelmed. He found renewed energy, and his productivity improved without the burden of constant stress. This experience taught Ravi a vital lesson: commitment is valuable, but it should never come at the expense of one's health and personal life.

Understanding Performance Pressure

The story of Ravi highlights a common yet often overlooked workplace issue: overburdening reliable employees. When managers recognize someone as dependable, they tend to delegate extra responsibilities to them, unintentionally creating a cycle where the employee becomes increasingly overloaded. Over time, this leads to exhaustion, burnout, and a decline in both physical and mental health. The employee, like Ravi, might start questioning their own worth and competence as they struggle to keep up with escalating demands.

For organizations, relying heavily on a select few can create an imbalance in the team. Not only does it place unnecessary pressure on certain individuals, but it also creates a high risk of turnover. Managers should be mindful of distributing workloads fairly and regularly check in with team members to ensure they aren't overwhelmed. Employees, on the other hand, need to cultivate self-awareness, set boundaries, and communicate openly about their capacities. Knowing when to step back, delegate, or even decline additional work can preserve long-term productivity and well-being.

Techniques for Managing Performance Pressure

1. **Communicate Openly with Management**

   Ravi realized he needed to have a candid conversation with his manager about the expectations being set. He prepared for the meeting by collecting data on previous performance metrics and suggested more achievable goals. This proactive communication opened the door for a constructive discussion about workload and realistic targets.

2. **Set Personal Goals**

Instead of solely focusing on management's expectations, Ravi began setting his personal, achievable goals aligned with his strengths and capacities. This shift allowed him to regain a sense of control over his work and celebrate small wins.

3. **Prioritize Tasks Effectively**

To manage his workload, Ravi adopted prioritization techniques like the Eisenhower Matrix, which helped him distinguish between urgent and important tasks. This method reduced his feelings of being overwhelmed by allowing him to focus on what truly mattered.

4. **Practice Stress-Reduction Techniques**

Ravi began incorporating stress-reduction techniques into his routine, such as mindfulness meditation and deep-breathing exercises. These practices helped him maintain calm and clarity amidst pressure, allowing him to approach challenges with a balanced mindset.

5. **Seek Support from Colleagues**

Understanding that he wasn't alone in this struggle, Ravi reached out to his colleagues to form a support network. They shared their experiences and coping strategies, which fostered a sense of community and collective resilience.

Reflections and Exercises

- **Reflection Prompt**: How do you respond to performance pressure in your job? What strategies have you tried, and how effective were they?

- **Journal Exercise**: Write about a time you felt overwhelmed by expectations. What steps can you take to address this in the future?

- **Affirmation**: "I manage performance pressure effectively. I set realistic goals and prioritize my well-being."

Takeaways from Ravi's Story

1. **Set Healthy Boundaries**: Commitment is important, but without clear boundaries, overwork can take a serious toll on health. Learning to set boundaries early on helps avoid burnout.

2. **Communicate Openly with Supervisors**: When the workload becomes overwhelming, being honest with supervisors can lead to constructive solutions. Managers are often willing to adjust responsibilities if they understand the impact on their team.

3. **Prioritize Self-Care and Balance**: A successful career should not come at the cost of mental and physical health. Recognizing the need for balance and practicing self-care can sustain long-term productivity.

4. **Seek Support from Mentors or Colleagues**: Talking to a mentor or a trusted colleague can provide perspective and practical advice for managing stress and workload.

5. **Understand Your Limits and Value**: Being reliable is valuable, but so is recognizing your own limits. Knowing your worth isn't tied to constantly proving yourself with endless tasks.

Ravi's journey reminds us that dedication and ambition are important qualities, but they should be balanced with respect for one's well-being. By setting boundaries and being open about capacity, both employees and employers can create a healthier, more sustainable work environment.

Chapter 22: Struggling with Lack of Recognition or Appreciation

Story of Neha: The Unsung Hero

Neha had always prided herself on being a diligent and detail-oriented employee at her marketing firm. As a senior marketing executive, she was instrumental in executing successful campaigns and driving impressive results. Her efforts often went unnoticed, overshadowed by the more vocal and flamboyant members of her team. While her colleagues often received accolades for their contributions, Neha felt like a shadow, continuously working hard but rarely receiving recognition or appreciation.

In meetings, she often found herself sitting quietly, listening as others presented their ideas. Her thoughtful suggestions were frequently overlooked or claimed by more assertive colleagues. Neha had developed a habit of second-guessing herself, doubting the value of her insights. As the months rolled by, her frustration grew, and she started to question her place in the team. Why did her hard work seem invisible? Did her colleagues not see the effort she put in behind the scenes?

One day, during a team meeting, the project manager announced that the company would be presenting awards to top performers for the quarter. This stirred mixed emotions in Neha. While she was happy for her colleagues who were always in the spotlight, a sense of discontent simmered beneath her surface. After the meeting, she confided in her friend and coworker, Samira, about her feelings of being undervalued. Samira encouraged Neha to speak up about her contributions and to advocate for herself more effectively.

Taking Samira's advice to heart, Neha made a list of her accomplishments and contributions over the past year, including successful campaigns, increased client satisfaction ratings, and innovative strategies she had implemented. Armed with this information, Neha decided to schedule a one-on-one meeting with her manager to discuss her concerns. She approached the conversation with a mix of anxiety and determination, ready to advocate for herself and her contributions.

During the meeting, Neha expressed her feelings of being overlooked despite her hard work. She shared her accomplishments and the value she brought to the team. To her surprise, her manager listened attentively, acknowledging Neha's contributions and expressing regret for not recognizing her efforts sooner. Her manager emphasized that it wasn't intentional but a byproduct of the busy work environment. He promised to ensure that her achievements would be highlighted in future meetings and recognized in performance reviews.

Encouraged by this positive response, Neha began to take more initiative in team discussions. She started to voice her ideas confidently and position herself as a key player in upcoming projects. Over time, her colleagues began to take notice of her contributions. The more she shared her insights, the more they began to value her perspective.

As the next quarterly performance review approached, Neha was nervous but hopeful. When the time came, she was thrilled to receive an award for her outstanding contributions to the team. The recognition not only boosted her confidence but also shifted the dynamic in the workplace. She learned the importance of advocating for herself and the value of speaking up for her worth.

Understanding the Importance of Recognition

Neha's story illustrates the struggles many employees face in workplaces where self-promotion and visibility often overshadow hard work. The feeling of being an "unsung hero" can lead to frustration, decreased motivation, and a lack of recognition. Often, employees like Neha pour their hearts into their work yet feel invisible due to their quieter demeanor or reluctance to self-advocate.

The story highlights the importance of recognizing and valuing all contributions, no matter how small they may seem. Managers should create an environment that encourages open communication and ensures that everyone has the opportunity to share their insights. Likewise, employees should feel empowered to advocate for themselves and highlight their accomplishments, understanding that self-promotion is not synonymous with arrogance.

Strategies for Seeking Recognition

1. **Advocate for Yourself**

   Neha learned to advocate for her achievements by documenting her contributions and successes. During team meetings, she made it a point to share her accomplishments, ensuring her efforts were acknowledged.

2. **Request Feedback**

Seeking feedback from her manager helped Neha understand how her work impacted the team. She scheduled regular one-on-one meetings to discuss her progress, allowing her to receive constructive criticism and recognition for her contributions.

3. **Build a Personal Brand**

Neha began to build her personal brand within the organization by showcasing her expertise through presentations and sharing insights during team discussions. This proactive approach not only increased her visibility but also established her as a valuable team member.

4. **Create a Culture of Appreciation**

Neha initiated informal recognition practices within her team. She encouraged her colleagues to express gratitude for each other's contributions, fostering a supportive environment where appreciation became a part of the team culture.

5. **Focus on Internal Validation**

While external recognition is important, Neha also worked on building her self-worth independently. She practiced self-affirmations and celebrated her achievements, reminding herself of her value beyond external validation.

Reflections and Exercises

- **Reflection Prompt**: How do you currently seek recognition in your workplace? Are there changes you can make to feel more valued?

- **Journal Exercise**: List three accomplishments from the past month that you are proud of. How can you share these with your team?

- **Affirmation**: "I am valuable and worthy of recognition. I celebrate my contributions and seek feedback to grow."

Takeaways from Neha's Story

1. **Self-Advocacy is Key**: It's essential to advocate for oneself in the workplace. Speaking up about accomplishments and contributions can lead to recognition and career growth.

2. **Value of Documentation**: Keeping track of achievements and contributions allows employees to present their case effectively when discussing performance with managers.

3. **Create an Open Environment**: Managers should foster an inclusive atmosphere where all team members feel comfortable sharing their ideas and insights.

4. **Recognize All Contributions**: Acknowledging the work of quieter team members is crucial. Every contribution, big or small, adds value to the team's success.

5. **Confidence Builds Recognition**: Building confidence in oneself and one's abilities can lead to greater visibility and appreciation in the workplace.

Neha's journey serves as a powerful reminder that hard work deserves recognition. By advocating for herself and openly communicating her value, she not only transformed her experience at work but also became an inspiration for her colleagues to do the same.

Chapter 23: Unspoken Battles: Confronting Sexual Harassment and Mental Health in the Workplace

Story of Ananya: Navigating Sexual Harassment and Mental Health at Work

Ananya had always been passionate about her job as a project manager at a renowned tech firm. She loved leading her team, meeting deadlines, and exceeding client expectations. However, her enthusiasm began to dwindle when she became the target of unwanted advances from her immediate supervisor, Vikram.

Initially, Ananya brushed off Vikram's comments as harmless flirtation, convincing herself that it was a compliment. He would often compliment her on her appearance or make suggestive jokes during team meetings, and at first, she didn't think much of it. However, his behavior soon escalated. He started to make unwelcome physical contact—placing his hand on her shoulder or standing too close for comfort during discussions. Ananya felt increasingly uneasy, and the excitement she once felt for her job began to fade.

As Vikram's advances grew more persistent, Ananya felt trapped. She was afraid to report his behavior to HR, fearing it would affect her career and reputation. She became hyper-aware of her surroundings, constantly on guard whenever he was near. The stress of managing both the harassment and her workload began to take a toll on her mental health. Ananya found herself feeling anxious, irritable, and unable to concentrate on her tasks. Her once-flourishing work performance began to suffer, and her relationships with colleagues became strained as she withdrew from social interactions.

One evening, feeling overwhelmed, Ananya decided to confide in her friend Priya, who also worked at the same company. Priya listened empathetically and shared her own experience with workplace harassment. She encouraged Ananya to take action, emphasizing that no one should have to tolerate such behavior. With Priya's support, Ananya felt empowered to confront the issue.

The next day, Ananya documented all instances of Vikram's inappropriate behavior, noting dates, times, and specific comments he had made. She sought guidance from HR and learned about the company's policy on harassment. With Priya by her side, she approached the HR manager to report Vikram's actions. To her relief, the HR manager took her concerns seriously and assured her that an investigation would be conducted promptly.

As the investigation unfolded, Ananya began to feel a mix of emotions. She was anxious about the potential outcomes, but also relieved that she was no longer bearing this burden alone. During this time, she also prioritized her mental health. She started practicing mindfulness and meditation, which helped her manage her anxiety and regain some control over her feelings. Ananya also sought therapy to address the emotional impact of the harassment and to build her self-esteem back up.

Through therapy, Ananya learned essential coping strategies, including:

1. **Setting Boundaries**: Ananya practiced setting clear boundaries with her supervisor. She learned how to assertively communicate her discomfort when he made inappropriate comments, using phrases like, "I prefer to keep our conversations professional."

2. **Journaling:** She began journaling her feelings and experiences, which allowed her to process her emotions and track her progress. This helped her reflect on her journey and gain clarity about her goals.

3. **Seeking Support**: Ananya surrounded herself with supportive friends and colleagues who uplifted her. She joined a support group for individuals who had faced similar experiences, which fostered a sense of community and understanding.

4. **Self-Care Practices**: Prioritizing self-care became crucial for Ananya. She engaged in activities that brought her joy, such as painting and yoga, which helped her unwind and reconnect with herself.

As the investigation progressed, Ananya felt increasingly empowered. The HR department found sufficient evidence to address Vikram's behavior, leading to disciplinary action. Though the process was challenging, she realized that standing up for herself was a significant step toward healing and reclaiming her power.

Understanding Sexual Harassment and Its Impact

Ananya's story highlights the profound impact sexual harassment can have on mental health in the workplace. It illustrates how harassment can create a toxic environment, leading to anxiety, stress, and isolation. Ananya's experience reflects the reality many individuals face when confronted with such situations, where fear and uncertainty can prevent them from taking action.

Strategies and Exercises

1. **Documenting Incidents**: Keeping a detailed record of harassment incidents can be vital in reporting to HR or legal authorities. This documentation provides a factual basis for claims and helps individuals articulate their experiences clearly.

2. **Building a Support System:** Connecting with trusted colleagues, friends, or support groups can offer emotional relief and practical advice. Sharing experiences can validate feelings and reduce the sense of isolation.

3. **Practicing Self-Care**: Engaging in self-care routines can mitigate stress. Activities like exercise, meditation, or hobbies promote mental well-being and help individuals cope with the emotional fallout of harassment.

4. **Professional Support**: Seeking therapy or counseling can help individuals process trauma and develop coping strategies. Professional guidance can also enhance self-esteem and resilience.

5. **Understanding Rights**: Educating oneself about workplace policies regarding harassment is crucial. Knowing one's rights can empower individuals to take appropriate action when faced with inappropriate behavior.

Takeaway from Ananya's Story

1. **Empowerment through Action**: Taking action against harassment, though daunting, can lead to empowerment and healing. Reporting incidents can initiate change and create safer environments.

2. **Mental Health Matters**: Prioritizing mental health is essential, especially in the face of adversity. Implementing self-care strategies and seeking professional help can significantly aid recovery.

3. **Speak Up:** Open communication about experiences can break the silence surrounding harassment. Sharing stories can inspire others to come forward and seek help.

4. **Support Systems are Vital**: Building a network of supportive individuals can provide comfort and encouragement during challenging times. A strong support system can help individuals feel less alone in their struggles.

Ananya's journey serves as a powerful reminder of the importance of addressing sexual harassment in the workplace. By taking decisive action and prioritizing mental health, individuals can navigate these challenges and emerge stronger, paving the way for a healthier and more supportive work environment.

Chapter 24: Managing Anxiety in High-Stakes Work Environments

Story of Karan: The Anxious Achiever

Karan was the quintessential high performer. With an impressive resume and accolades adorning his office walls, he was often regarded as the star employee in his organization. His colleagues admired his work ethic, and management frequently praised him for exceeding targets and driving results. However, behind this façade of success lay a constant, gnawing anxiety that Karan struggled to manage.

Karan's anxiety began to escalate as his company prepared for a high-stakes project that would be showcased to top executives and stakeholders. The pressure to perform was immense, and the stakes had never been higher. He found himself lying awake at night, ruminating about potential failures and fearing the possibility of disappointing his team and leadership. As the project's launch date approached, Karan became increasingly withdrawn, skipping social gatherings and spending hours in front of his computer screen.

Despite his achievements, Karan felt like a fraud, grappling with feelings of inadequacy that gnawed at his self-esteem. He would often compare himself to his peers, convinced that everyone else was more competent and less anxious than he was. This imposter syndrome only amplified his stress and anxiety.

During a particularly challenging week, Karan had a panic attack while working late in the office. His heart raced, palms sweated, and he struggled to catch his breath. It was a wake-up call for him, as he realized that he could no longer ignore the toll his anxiety was taking on his mental health. After this incident, Karan sought help from a therapist who specialized in anxiety management and workplace stress.

Understanding Workplace Anxiety

Karan's experience highlights a critical aspect of workplace dynamics: the often-overlooked connection between high performance and mental health. In high-stakes environments, the pressure to succeed can lead to significant anxiety, resulting in a cycle that compromises both performance and mental well-being. Understanding the root causes of anxiety in the workplace is essential for both employees and organizations.

1. **High Expectations:** Employees like Karan often face unrealistic expectations from management, leading to increased stress levels. The pressure to deliver results can create a toxic cycle of overworking and anxiety.

2. **Comparison Culture:** The tendency to compare oneself to colleagues can exacerbate feelings of inadequacy. Karan's perception that his peers were more competent only fueled his anxiety.

3. **Imposter Syndrome:** Many high achievers struggle with imposter syndrome, feeling undeserving of their success. This can lead to burnout as they strive to maintain an illusion of competence.

4. **Lack of Support:** A workplace that lacks adequate support systems can leave employees feeling isolated in their struggles, increasing the risk of mental health challenges.

Anxiety Management Techniques

1. Practice Mindfulness and Meditation

Karan began incorporating mindfulness practices into his daily routine. Simple techniques, such as focusing on his breath or practicing gratitude, helped ground him during stressful moments.

2. Develop Organizational Skills

To combat feelings of overwhelm, Karan improved his organizational skills by creating detailed project plans and timelines. This proactive approach reduced uncertainty and allowed him to tackle tasks more efficiently.

3. Use Positive Visualization

Karan employed positive visualization techniques before important presentations or deadlines. By picturing himself succeeding, he cultivated a sense of confidence that helped alleviate anxiety.

4. Establish a Support System

Karan reached out to colleagues and friends to create a support network. Sharing experiences and strategies for coping with anxiety made him feel less isolated and more empowered.

5. **Seek Professional Help**

   Recognizing that he needed additional support, Karan sought the guidance of a therapist who specialized in workplace anxiety. Together, they developed tailored coping strategies and addressed underlying concerns.

Reflections and Exercises

- **Reflection Prompt**: How does anxiety affect your performance in high-stakes situations? What techniques have you tried to manage it?

- **Journal Exercise**: List three coping strategies you want to implement to manage anxiety. Create a plan for incorporating them into your daily routine.

- **Affirmation**: "I manage anxiety effectively. I cultivate calm and confidence in high-pressure situations."

Takeaway:

Karan's journey emphasizes the importance of recognizing and addressing anxiety in high-stakes work environments. Employees should feel empowered to communicate their challenges, seek support, and adopt strategies for managing stress. Organizations can play a pivotal role by fostering a culture that prioritizes mental well-being, allowing employees to thrive without compromising their health.

By understanding that anxiety is a common struggle, employees can work toward dismantling the stigma surrounding mental health, creating a more supportive and productive workplace for everyone.

Chapter 25: Returning to Work After a Personal Crisis

Story of Maya: The Resilient Return

Maya was a dedicated marketing executive, known for her creativity and passion for her work. She loved her job and the team she worked with, thriving in an environment that encouraged innovation and collaboration. However, her world turned upside down when she faced a devastating personal tragedy: the sudden loss of her mother to a terminal illness. The grief was overwhelming, and Maya found herself struggling to cope with the emotional fallout.

For weeks, she felt lost and unable to focus on anything, including her work. The deep sorrow made it difficult for her to engage in even the simplest tasks. Meetings felt unbearable, and the thought of returning to the office filled her with anxiety. To cope, Maya took a leave of absence, hoping that time away would help her process her grief and gather the strength to face her responsibilities again.

During her time off, Maya spent a lot of time reflecting on her life and the impact her mother had on her. She remembered her mother's resilience in the face of adversity and the lessons she had imparted about finding strength within oneself. Slowly, Maya began to channel her grief into a desire to honor her mother's memory by living fully and authentically.

After several weeks, Maya decided it was time to return to work. However, she felt apprehensive about how her colleagues would perceive her absence. Would they see her as weak? Would they understand her struggles? The fear of judgment loomed over her as she prepared to step back into the office.

On her first day back, Maya was greeted warmly by her team. They had missed her, and the genuine expressions of support helped ease her nerves. Her manager took the time to check in, acknowledging her loss and reassuring her that it was okay to take time to adjust. This empathetic approach provided Maya with the comfort she needed to begin reintegrating into her role.

Initially, Maya struggled with her workload, finding it difficult to concentrate during meetings or keep up with deadlines. However, she realized that she needed to set realistic expectations for herself. With her manager's support, she gradually adjusted her workload, prioritizing tasks that were manageable and allowing herself the grace to ease back into her routine.

Understanding the Impact of Personal Crises

Maya's experience sheds light on several critical aspects of returning to work after a personal crisis. The complexity of grief plays a significant role, as grieving is not a linear process, and everyone copes differently. Maya struggled to reconcile her overwhelming sorrow with the expectations of her professional life, revealing how challenging it can be to navigate emotional turmoil while managing work responsibilities. This underscores the necessity of having supportive workplace systems in place. Maya's journey highlighted the impact of a compassionate work environment; the empathy shown by her manager and colleagues was instrumental in easing her transition back into her role. Setting realistic expectations for oneself is crucial during this period. Maya learned to prioritize manageable tasks and allowed herself the grace to ease back into her routine, recognizing that her limits had changed.

Moreover, her journey emphasizes the importance of emotional resilience. By channeling her grief into a commitment to honor her mother's legacy, Maya discovered a renewed sense of purpose that fueled her return to work. Finally, effective communication is key in such scenarios. Maya's willingness to share her struggles with her colleagues fostered understanding and created a more compassionate workplace. Her story serves as a powerful reminder that while the path to recovery after a personal tragedy is fraught with challenges, it is also an opportunity for personal growth and renewed purpose. Organizations that nurture a culture of empathy not only support their employees' well-being but also contribute to a more engaged and productive workforce. Ultimately, Maya's journey demonstrates that returning to work is not merely about regaining productivity; it is about embracing one's journey, honoring the past, and finding strength in vulnerability.

Strategies for a Smooth Transition

1. **Communicate with Your Employer**

   Maya scheduled a meeting with her manager to discuss her return. She openly shared her feelings and the support she needed during the transition, allowing for an understanding and accommodating approach.

2. **Set Realistic Expectations**

Understanding her emotional state, Maya set realistic expectations for her workload. She prioritized essential tasks and gradually eased back into her responsibilities.

3. **Practice Self-Compassion**

Maya reminded herself that healing takes time. She practiced self-compassion, allowing herself to experience emotions without guilt or pressure to perform at her previous level.

4. **Establish a Support System at Work**

Maya sought support from her colleagues, sharing her experiences and feelings with trusted team members. This openness helped her feel more connected and less isolated during her transition.

5. **Engage in Stress-Relief Activities**

To manage stress and anxiety, Maya engaged in activities that brought her joy and relaxation, such as yoga and journaling. These practices provided her with the necessary outlets for her emotions.

Reflections and Exercises

- **Reflection Prompt**: How do personal crises affect your work life? What strategies have you found helpful in navigating these challenges?

- **Journal Exercise**: Write about your feelings as you return to work after a difficult time. What support do you need from your colleagues?

- **Affirmation**: "I embrace my journey of healing. I am patient with myself as I return to work."

Takeaway:

Maya's story is a powerful reminder of the resilience of the human spirit in the face of loss. It highlights the importance of support systems in the workplace and the value of compassion when helping colleagues navigate personal crises. Organizations that foster a culture of understanding and empathy not only contribute to their employees' well-being but also create a more engaged and productive workforce.

By sharing her experience, Maya encourages others to seek help and support during difficult times. Her journey demonstrates that while the path to recovery may be fraught with challenges, it is also paved with opportunities for personal growth and renewed purpose. The ability to return to work after a personal tragedy is not merely about regaining productivity; it is about embracing one's journey, honoring the past, and finding strength in vulnerability.

Chapter 26: Supporting a Colleague Facing Mental Health Issues

Story of Rahul: The Supportive Teammate

Rahul had always been known as the go-to person on his team. He was the one who would lend a helping hand to anyone in need, whether it was tackling a challenging project or providing emotional support. When his colleague, Arjun, began showing signs of distress, Rahul sensed something was wrong. Arjun, once enthusiastic and engaged, had become withdrawn and often missed deadlines. Concerned for his friend, Rahul decided to reach out.

One afternoon, during a casual coffee break, Rahul approached Arjun. He opened up about how he had noticed changes in Arjun's behavior, expressing genuine concern for his well-being. "Hey, I've noticed you seem a bit off lately," Rahul said softly. "If you ever want to talk about anything, I'm here for you." Arjun, initially hesitant, felt the warmth of Rahul's support and eventually opened up about the overwhelming stress he had been experiencing, not just from work but also from personal issues.

Recognizing the importance of creating a safe space, Rahul listened without judgment, allowing Arjun to express his feelings. He shared his own experiences of stress and anxiety, illustrating that it was normal to feel overwhelmed sometimes. This sharing of experiences helped Arjun feel less isolated in his struggles. Encouraged by their conversation, Rahul suggested practical strategies for managing stress, such as taking regular breaks, practicing mindfulness techniques, and seeking professional support if needed.

As their conversations continued, Rahul made a conscious effort to check in on Arjun regularly. He encouraged him to engage in team activities and suggested ways to manage workload better. With this support, Arjun slowly began to regain his confidence. He started to participate more actively in team meetings and even volunteered for a few projects. Over time, he became more open about his struggles with the team, which not only helped him but also inspired others to share their challenges, fostering a culture of support within the team.

Understanding the Role of Support in Mental Health

Rahul's story illustrates the profound impact that one supportive colleague can have on another's mental health and overall well-being in the workplace. His proactive approach to reaching out to Arjun exemplifies the importance of awareness and empathy in identifying signs of distress in coworkers. Creating a safe space for open conversations can significantly reduce feelings of isolation that often accompany mental health struggles.

Moreover, Rahul's willingness to share his own experiences of stress normalizes the conversation around mental health, making it easier for others to open up. It underscores the idea that vulnerability can foster deeper connections among colleagues, encouraging a culture where discussing mental health is not stigmatized but rather embraced.

Supportive actions, such as regular check-ins and practical suggestions for coping strategies, demonstrate that the workplace can be a community that prioritizes mental wellness. Rahul's approach of combining emotional support with actionable advice exemplifies how colleagues can empower each other to seek help and implement positive changes in their lives.

Offering support to a colleague facing mental health issues is crucial for fostering a positive workplace environment. It requires sensitivity, understanding, and the ability to maintain boundaries.

Strategies for Offering Support

1. **Initiate a Private Conversation**

   Rahul approached Aisha in a private setting, expressing his concern for her well-being. He listened attentively as she shared her feelings, creating a safe space for her to open up.

2. **Use Empathetic Language**

   Rahul practiced empathy by validating Aisha's feelings and experiences. He avoided minimizing her struggles and instead offered a compassionate perspective.

3. **Encourage Professional Help**

Rahul gently encouraged Aisha to consider seeking professional help, providing information about available resources. He made it clear that seeking help is a sign of strength, not weakness.

4. **Respect Boundaries**

While offering support, Rahul respected Aisha's boundaries, ensuring that he didn't pry into her personal life or push her to share more than she was comfortable with.

5. **Foster a Positive Team Environment**

Rahul advocated for a supportive team culture by promoting mental health awareness within the workplace. He initiated discussions about mental health resources and encouraged open communication among team members.

Reflections and Exercises

- **Reflection Prompt**: Have you ever supported a colleague in distress? What did you learn from the experience?

- **Journal Exercise**: Reflect on a time when you received support during a challenging period. How did it make you feel, and how can you extend that support to others?

- **Affirmation**: "I offer support with compassion and respect. I create a safe space for my colleagues to share their experiences."

Takeaway

The key takeaway from Rahul's story is the importance of fostering a supportive work environment where employees feel safe to share their struggles. By being attentive and compassionate, colleagues can make a significant difference in each other's lives. Small gestures of support, such as listening without judgment, offering encouragement, and sharing personal experiences, can create a ripple effect, ultimately leading to a more engaged, resilient, and cohesive workplace. In an era where mental health is increasingly recognized as a vital aspect of overall well-being, the role of supportive teammates like Rahul becomes essential in cultivating a culture of empathy and understanding.

Chapter 27: Gender Dynamics and Workplace Bias

Story of Priya: Navigating Bias in a Male-Dominated Field

Priya was a talented engineer with a passion for innovation and problem-solving. After completing her degree in engineering with top honors, she secured a job at a leading tech firm known for its cutting-edge projects and strong team dynamics. Excited about her new role, Priya was eager to contribute her skills and bring fresh ideas to the table. However, she quickly discovered that the reality of working in a male-dominated field posed unexpected challenges.

From her first day, Priya noticed subtle biases in her interactions with colleagues. Meetings often turned into sessions where her contributions were overlooked or dismissed, while male colleagues received enthusiastic nods and praise for similar ideas. Comments about her appearance or assumptions about her capabilities based on her gender were not uncommon, leaving Priya feeling frustrated and undervalued. Despite her qualifications and expertise, she often felt she had to prove herself more than her male counterparts.

Determined not to let bias define her career, Priya sought ways to navigate this challenging environment. She began documenting her contributions meticulously, ensuring that her work was visible and recognized. During meetings, she made it a point to assertively voice her ideas, often following up with supportive data or examples to reinforce her points. Over time, she learned to address dismissive comments with confidence, responding with well-reasoned arguments that underscored her competence.

Recognizing the importance of allies, Priya also made an effort to build relationships with other women in her field and sought mentorship from female leaders within the organization. She attended networking events and workshops aimed at empowering women in tech, which not only expanded her professional circle but also provided her with a sense of community and shared experiences. These connections proved invaluable, as they offered insights on overcoming challenges and navigating workplace dynamics effectively.

As Priya gained confidence and built a supportive network, she began to notice a shift in how her colleagues perceived her. Her colleagues started to respect her contributions more, and some even sought her input on critical projects. Priya's perseverance and commitment to excellence led her to be recognized in the company's quarterly meeting for her innovative solutions to a challenging engineering problem, a moment that solidified her place within the team.

Understanding Gender Dynamics in the Workplace

Priya's experience highlights the pervasive issue of gender bias in male-dominated industries and its impact on women's professional development. Bias can manifest in various forms, from overt discrimination to subtle microaggressions that can undermine a woman's confidence and contributions. The challenges Priya faced serve as a reminder of the systemic barriers that many women encounter in their careers, often requiring them to navigate complex dynamics to assert their presence and capabilities.

Priya's story underscores the importance of resilience and proactive strategies in combating bias. By documenting her work and assertively communicating her ideas, she was able to carve out a space for herself and establish her credibility. Additionally, building a supportive network of peers and mentors not only empowered Priya but also contributed to a broader movement toward fostering inclusivity within her workplace.

This narrative also highlights the role of organizations in addressing gender bias. By promoting diversity, offering mentorship programs, and fostering an inclusive culture, companies can create environments where women like Priya can thrive and contribute meaningfully without facing undue barriers. Priya's journey illustrates the potential for change when individuals advocate for themselves and seek to uplift others in similar situations.

Gender dynamics and biases can significantly affect women's experiences in the workplace. They can manifest as unequal pay, fewer opportunities for advancement, and a lack of recognition for contributions.

Strategies for Addressing Gender Bias

1. **Recognize and Document Instances of Bias**

   Priya began documenting instances of bias she encountered, including comments made in meetings or decisions that favored her male colleagues. This record served as evidence for discussions with management and helped her articulate her experiences clearly.

2. **Build a Support Network**

Priya connected with other women in her field through networking groups and mentorship programs. This network provided her with support, resources, and shared experiences, reinforcing her sense of belonging and empowerment.

3. **Develop Assertiveness Skills**

Priya worked on building her assertiveness by practicing how to voice her ideas and opinions confidently in meetings. She learned to speak up and advocate for herself without fear of being dismissed.

4. **Seek Mentorship and Sponsorship**

Understanding the value of mentorship, Priya actively sought out mentors within her organization. These mentors provided guidance, helped navigate workplace challenges, and advocated for her when opportunities arose.

5. **Promote Diversity and Inclusion Initiatives**

Priya took the initiative to participate in her company's diversity and inclusion committees. By contributing to these initiatives, she worked towards creating a more equitable workplace for everyone.

Reflections and Exercises

- **Reflection Prompt**: Have you experienced gender bias in your workplace? How did it impact your career, and what strategies did you use to cope?

- **Journal Exercise**: Write about a time you stood up against bias. What was the outcome, and how did it make you feel?

- **Affirmation**: "I am empowered to challenge gender biases. I advocate for myself and others in the workplace."

The key takeaway from Priya's story is the significance of resilience and advocacy in navigating gender bias in the workplace. By documenting achievements, asserting oneself in discussions, and building a network of support, women can challenge stereotypes and create pathways for their success. It also emphasizes the necessity for organizations to actively work towards inclusivity, recognizing the value that diverse perspectives bring to the table. In doing so, both individuals and companies can foster a culture where all employees feel valued, respected, and empowered to succeed, ultimately enriching the workplace for everyone.

Chapter 28: Managing Procrastination and Self-Discipline

Story of Rohan: The Chronic Procrastinator

Rohan was a bright, creative professional working in marketing at a well-known advertising agency. He had a natural flair for generating innovative ideas and a passion for his work. However, despite his talent, Rohan struggled with chronic procrastination that often derailed his projects and left him feeling overwhelmed. As deadlines approached, he found himself stuck in a cycle of last-minute work, stress, and frustration, which began to take a toll on his mental health.

Initially, Rohan thought he could manage his procrastination by working late nights or cramming right before deadlines. He rationalized his behavior by convincing himself that he worked better under pressure. However, as time went on, this approach led to increased anxiety and diminished quality in his work. Colleagues and supervisors noticed Rohan's inconsistent performance, which further fueled his self-doubt and feelings of inadequacy.

One day, after receiving feedback on a campaign that didn't meet expectations due to his rushed work, Rohan realized he needed to change his approach. Determined to break free from the cycle of procrastination, he started researching effective time management techniques. He discovered the Pomodoro Technique, which involved working in focused bursts with short breaks in between. Rohan decided to implement this method, breaking his projects into smaller, manageable tasks. This allowed him to tackle his work without feeling overwhelmed and helped him regain a sense of control.

Rohan also set specific goals and deadlines for himself, using a planner to track his progress. He began prioritizing tasks based on urgency and importance, which helped him focus on what truly mattered. To stay accountable, he shared his goals with a trusted colleague, who supported him in maintaining his progress. Rohan found that this open communication not only kept him accountable but also strengthened his professional relationships.

As Rohan started to implement these changes, he noticed a remarkable difference in his productivity and mental well-being. He completed tasks ahead of schedule, which reduced his stress and gave him time to refine his ideas. His newfound organization and efficiency allowed him to participate more actively in brainstorming sessions, contributing creatively without the cloud of impending deadlines. His confidence grew as his work quality improved, and he earned recognition for his contributions during team meetings.

Understanding Procrastination

Rohan's story illustrates the pervasive issue of procrastination and its significant impact on personal and professional life. Procrastination can stem from various factors, including fear of failure, perfectionism, and poor time management skills. For Rohan, the habit of putting off tasks created a cycle of stress and anxiety, undermining his confidence and hindering his performance. His experience highlights the emotional toll of procrastination, emphasizing the importance of addressing the root causes rather than merely managing the symptoms.

Moreover, Rohan's journey demonstrates that overcoming procrastination is not merely about time management; it is about fostering a mindset shift. By recognizing that he needed to change his approach, Rohan embraced strategies that helped him cultivate discipline and accountability. His proactive steps, such as breaking tasks into smaller components and sharing goals with a colleague, were crucial in reshaping his work habits.

This narrative underscores the importance of seeking support and developing strategies tailored to individual needs. By experimenting with different techniques and finding what worked for him, Rohan was able to create a system that fostered productivity and reduced anxiety. His journey emphasizes that overcoming procrastination requires commitment, self-awareness, and a willingness to adopt new habits.

Strategies for Overcoming Procrastination

1. **Identify Triggers**

   Rohan started by identifying what triggered his procrastination. He noticed that large projects overwhelmed him, causing him to avoid starting them. Understanding these triggers allowed him to address them directly.

2. **Break Tasks into Smaller Steps**

To make tasks more manageable, Rohan broke his projects into smaller, actionable steps. This technique helped him focus on one task at a time, reducing the feeling of being overwhelmed.

3. **Establish a Routine**

Rohan created a daily routine that included specific time blocks for focused work. This structure helped him build discipline and minimize distractions during work hours.

4. **Set Clear Deadlines**

He set personal deadlines for himself that were earlier than actual due dates. By creating this buffer, Rohan allowed himself time for unexpected challenges and reduced last-minute stress.

5. **Utilize Time Management Techniques**

Rohan experimented with time management techniques like the Pomodoro Technique, where he worked for 25 minutes followed by a 5-minute break. This method increased his focus and productivity.

Reflections and Exercises

- **Reflection Prompt**: What are your primary reasons for procrastination? How do they impact your work and personal life?

- **Journal Exercise**: List three tasks you've been procrastinating. Break them down into smaller steps and create a plan to tackle them.

- **Affirmation**: "I take control of my time and actions. I am disciplined and proactive in my work."

Takeaway

The key takeaway from Rohan's story is the understanding that procrastination is a common struggle that can significantly impact personal and professional success. It highlights the necessity of addressing underlying factors contributing to procrastination, such as fear and poor time management. By implementing effective strategies like the Pomodoro Technique, setting clear goals, and fostering accountability through support systems, individuals can break free from the cycle of procrastination and enhance their productivity and well-being. Ultimately, Rohan's experience serves as a reminder that positive change is possible through self-reflection, determination, and the willingness to seek out and implement effective solutions.

Chapter 29: Dealing with Job Role Ambiguity

Story of Aisha: The Confused Employee

Aisha was a recent graduate who had landed her first job as a project coordinator at a fast-paced tech company. Excited to begin her professional journey, she quickly realized that the reality of the workplace was far more complex than she had anticipated. While she was eager to contribute, Aisha found herself grappling with confusion regarding her role and responsibilities. The company culture was dynamic, and the expectations seemed to shift frequently, leaving her feeling lost and overwhelmed.

In her first few weeks, Aisha attended numerous meetings where discussions revolved around various projects, but she often felt out of the loop. Her supervisor, while knowledgeable, was not very communicative about specific tasks or expectations. As a result, Aisha struggled to understand what was expected of her, leading to anxiety about her performance. She wanted to ask questions but feared that doing so might expose her lack of knowledge or make her seem incompetent.

Over time, this confusion took a toll on Aisha's confidence. She began to doubt her capabilities, which affected her enthusiasm for her work. Feeling isolated, she hesitated to reach out to her colleagues for help, thinking they might view her as inadequate. Instead, she tried to navigate her role on her own, leading to mistakes and missed deadlines, which further compounded her feelings of self-doubt.

One day, during a team meeting, Aisha's supervisor encouraged open communication and invited team members to voice any concerns about their roles. Gathering her courage, Aisha took a leap of faith and expressed her struggles with understanding her responsibilities. To her surprise, several colleagues chimed in, sharing that they too had faced similar feelings of confusion when they started. This moment of vulnerability fostered a sense of camaraderie among the team and prompted her supervisor to provide more structured guidance.

Aisha's supervisor then organized a series of one-on-one meetings with team members to clarify roles and expectations. During her session, Aisha learned about the importance of open communication and actively seeking clarification when needed. She discussed her projects, expressed her uncertainties, and gained valuable insights from her colleagues, which helped demystify her position within the team.

Armed with new knowledge and a supportive network, Aisha began to approach her work differently. She started asking questions without fear of judgment and sought feedback on her tasks. By clarifying expectations and understanding her role better, Aisha regained her confidence and began to excel in her projects. She learned to prioritize her tasks and even took the initiative to create a shared document that outlined project responsibilities, which benefited not only her but also her team members.

Understanding Job Role Ambiguity

Aisha's story highlights the detrimental effects of role ambiguity and confusion in the workplace. When employees lack clarity about their responsibilities, it can lead to feelings of inadequacy, anxiety, and decreased job satisfaction. Aisha's initial struggle with understanding her role is a common experience for many employees, especially those in dynamic and fast-paced environments. This confusion can hinder productivity and contribute to a toxic work culture where employees feel unsupported.

The turning point in Aisha's journey came when she found the courage to communicate her struggles openly. This pivotal moment underscores the importance of fostering a workplace culture that encourages open dialogue. By creating an environment where employees feel safe to express their uncertainties, organizations can promote collaboration and build stronger teams. Aisha's experience also illustrates the value of mentorship and peer support in helping employees navigate their roles effectively.

Furthermore, Aisha's initiative to create a shared document for project responsibilities reflects a proactive approach to addressing role ambiguity. It emphasizes the need for clear communication channels and structured frameworks within teams to ensure everyone is aligned. This collaborative effort not only clarified responsibilities but also enhanced team cohesion, showcasing how teamwork can alleviate confusion and improve overall performance.

Strategies for Clarifying Job Roles

1. **Initiate Conversations with Supervisors**

   Aisha scheduled a meeting with her supervisor to discuss her concerns about role clarity. She prepared a list of questions to ensure she covered all aspects of her job responsibilities.

2. **Create a Job Description Outline**

   After her meeting, Aisha drafted an outline of her job description based on her understanding and supervisor's input. This outline served as a reference for her daily tasks and responsibilities.

3. **Seek Feedback Regularly**

   Aisha made it a habit to seek feedback from her supervisor and colleagues. Regular check-ins provided her with clarity on her performance and allowed her to adjust her approach as needed.

4. **Establish Clear Goals**

   Aisha worked with her supervisor to set specific, measurable goals for her role. These goals provided direction and helped her understand what was expected of her.

5. **Document Responsibilities**

   To keep track of her responsibilities, Aisha maintained a log of her daily tasks and accomplishments. This documentation helped her identify areas where she excelled and where she needed improvement.

Reflections and Exercises

- **Reflection Prompt**: Have you ever experienced job role ambiguity? How did it affect your performance and job satisfaction?

- **Journal Exercise**: Write down your current job responsibilities. Are there areas that feel unclear? How can you seek clarification?

- **Affirmation**: "I seek clarity in my role and responsibilities. I communicate effectively to ensure my contributions are valued."

Takeaway

The key takeaway from Aisha's story is the recognition that role ambiguity can have profound effects on employee confidence, performance, and overall job satisfaction. It highlights the necessity for organizations to cultivate a culture of open communication where employees feel comfortable seeking clarification and support. By addressing role confusion proactively and encouraging collaborative efforts, organizations can foster an environment that promotes engagement and productivity.

Ultimately, Aisha's journey illustrates that overcoming confusion in the workplace is possible through open dialogue, supportive mentorship, and a willingness to take initiative. By prioritizing clear communication and collaboration, both employees and organizations can create a more positive and effective work environment where everyone can thrive.

Chapter 30: Addressing Workplace Jealousy and Comparison

Story of Shubham: The Jealous Colleague

Shubham had always been a high achiever, known for his hard work and dedication. He prided himself on being the go-to person for solving problems at his job in a marketing firm. However, when a new colleague, Priya, joined the team, Shubham's feelings began to shift. Priya was not only talented but also quickly earned the admiration of their manager and the respect of their peers. As she contributed innovative ideas during team meetings, Shubham couldn't help but feel a pang of jealousy.

Initially, he tried to shake off these feelings, rationalizing that everyone had their strengths. However, as Priya received praise for her work, Shubham's jealousy began to fester. He found himself growing resentful of her successes, and this negativity affected his mood and performance. He started to compare himself to her constantly, scrutinizing every presentation she gave and every compliment she received.

This sense of competition drove Shubham to work harder, but instead of channeling his energy into self-improvement, he began undermining Priya subtly. He made snide comments about her ideas during meetings, dismissing them without giving them proper consideration. When the team celebrated Priya's achievements, Shubham would feign enthusiasm while feeling bitter inside.

His behavior did not go unnoticed. His colleagues started to perceive a tension between him and Priya, and it created an uncomfortable atmosphere within the team. Over time, Shubham's growing negativity and resentment not only impacted his relationship with Priya but also affected the morale of the entire team. He became increasingly isolated, while Priya continued to thrive, oblivious to the internal struggle Shubham faced.

Eventually, a senior manager called Shubham in for a candid conversation. Noticing his declining performance and attitude, she pointed out that his jealousy was not only harming his work but also affecting the team dynamics. She encouraged him to reflect on what he valued in his work and how he could use Priya's success as inspiration rather than a source of envy.

Taking this advice to heart, Shubham began to introspect. He realized that his jealousy stemmed from insecurity about his own abilities. Instead of seeing Priya as a rival, he decided to view her as a colleague from whom he could learn. Shubham approached Priya, offering to collaborate on a project where they could share ideas and insights. To his surprise, she welcomed the collaboration with open arms.

Working together, Shubham found that he could appreciate Priya's skills and creativity without feeling threatened. He learned to communicate openly with her about their work and to celebrate her achievements genuinely. Over time, this shift in perspective helped him regain his confidence and reignite his passion for his own work.

Understanding Workplace Jealousy

Shubham's story serves as a powerful illustration of how jealousy can disrupt workplace harmony and personal well-being. Jealousy, when left unchecked, can lead to negative behaviors that not only harm professional relationships but also undermine one's own self-esteem and performance. Shubham's initial response to jealousy—competition and sabotage—was counterproductive and ultimately detrimental to his career and mental health.

The turning point in Shubham's journey was his willingness to confront his feelings and seek help. This highlights the importance of self-awareness and the ability to reflect on one's emotions. Recognizing that jealousy was rooted in his own insecurities allowed him to shift his focus from comparison to collaboration. This transformation is crucial in fostering a positive work environment where team members support and uplift one another.

Shubham's decision to collaborate with Priya rather than compete against her emphasizes the value of teamwork and mutual respect in the workplace. It is essential for employees to understand that success does not have to come at the expense of others. By working together, individuals can leverage each other's strengths and create a more cohesive and productive team dynamic.

Strategies for Overcoming Jealousy

1. **Reframe Your Perspective**

Shubham learned to reframe his thoughts about his colleague's success. Instead of viewing it as a threat, he began to see it as an opportunity for learning and inspiration.

2. **Focus on Personal Growth**

Shubham shifted his focus from comparing himself to others to setting personal goals. He identified areas for improvement and worked towards achieving his aspirations without external comparisons.

3. **Celebrate Others' Successes**

To combat jealousy, Shubham made a conscious effort to celebrate his colleague's achievements. This shift in attitude helped him foster a supportive environment rather than one of competition.

4. **Practice Gratitude**

Shubham started a gratitude journal, writing down things he was thankful for, including his own accomplishments. This practice helped him appreciate his journey and reduced feelings of jealousy.

5. **Seek Collaboration**

Shubham reached out to his colleague for collaboration on a project. Working together not only strengthened their relationship but also allowed him to learn from her success.

Reflections and Exercises

- **Reflection Prompt**: How does jealousy affect your workplace relationships? What strategies can you employ to address these feelings?

- **Journal Exercise**: Identify a colleague you admire. What qualities do you appreciate about them? How can you incorporate those qualities into your work?

- **Affirmation**: "I celebrate the success of others. I focus on my journey and growth, free from comparison."

Takeaway

The key takeaway from Shubham's story is the recognition that jealousy in the workplace is a common but often destructive emotion. It can lead to feelings of isolation and resentment, negatively impacting both individual performance and team morale. The story underscores the necessity for individuals to cultivate self-awareness, recognize their emotions, and find constructive ways to address them.

Embracing collaboration over competition can lead to personal growth and a healthier work environment. By learning to celebrate the successes of others and viewing them as opportunities for learning rather than threats, employees can foster stronger relationships and enhance their overall job satisfaction. Ultimately, Shubham's journey illustrates that overcoming jealousy requires introspection, communication, and a commitment to building a supportive workplace culture.

Conclusion: Embracing Mental Health in the Workplace

In the dynamic landscape of modern work environments, the importance of mental health has emerged as a crucial component of overall well-being and productivity. As we have explored through various stories throughout this book, the challenges individuals face in the workplace—from navigating toxic relationships to overcoming feelings of inadequacy—are not isolated incidents but rather reflections of a broader issue that affects countless employees across different industries. It is essential to recognize that mental health is not merely an individual concern; it is a collective responsibility that organizations must prioritize.

The narratives presented in this book illustrate the complex interplay between mental health and workplace dynamics. Each story, whether it involves feelings of jealousy, anxiety, bias, or the struggle for work-life balance, reveals the profound impact that our work environment can have on our mental well-being. The experiences of characters like Shubham, Priya, and Maya highlight that mental health challenges are often exacerbated by organizational cultures that overlook the emotional and psychological needs of their employees. This recognition is the first step toward fostering a more inclusive and supportive workplace.

To embrace mental health in the workplace, organizations must take proactive steps to create a culture that prioritizes psychological safety and open dialogue. This involves implementing policies and practices that encourage employees to discuss their mental health concerns without fear of judgment or repercussion. Training programs focused on mental health awareness can equip employees and managers alike with the tools to recognize signs of distress and support one another effectively. It is vital to normalize conversations about mental health, making it clear that seeking help is a sign of strength rather than weakness.

Furthermore, organizations can benefit from incorporating mental health resources into their employee assistance programs. Access to counseling, mindfulness workshops, and stress management resources can empower employees to address their mental health needs proactively. Regular wellness check-ins, flexible work arrangements, and opportunities for professional development can also contribute to a healthier work-life balance, thereby reducing the risk of burnout and fostering resilience among employees.

As individuals, we also bear the responsibility of nurturing our mental health. The stories of characters like Anjali and Rohan remind us that self-awareness and self-care are critical components of maintaining well-being in the face of workplace challenges. Building resilience through mindfulness practices, setting boundaries, and seeking support when needed can help us navigate the complexities of our work lives more effectively.

It is essential to remember that mental health is not a destination but a continuous journey. The commitment to prioritizing mental well-being must extend beyond immediate interventions to encompass long-term cultural shifts within organizations. By fostering an environment that values mental health, we not only enhance employee satisfaction and retention but also boost productivity and innovation. Healthy employees are engaged employees, and their well-being directly correlates with an organization's success.

In conclusion, embracing mental health in the workplace is not just a trend but a necessity. It calls for a collaborative effort from organizations, leaders, and employees alike to cultivate an environment that recognizes, supports, and promotes mental well-being. As we move forward, let us commit to breaking the stigma surrounding mental health, sharing our stories, and advocating for change. By doing so, we can transform our workplaces into spaces where everyone feels valued, heard, and empowered to thrive. Together, we can build a future where mental health is a fundamental priority—because a healthy workplace is a thriving workplace.

The Importance of Mental Health Awareness

The workplace is more than just a venue for professional achievement; it is a space where individuals spend a significant portion of their lives. Mental health significantly impacts not only personal well-being but also organizational productivity and culture. When employees feel supported, understood, and empowered, they are more likely to thrive, innovate, and contribute meaningfully to their teams.

Through the stories of Aarav, Meera, Priya, Rohan, and many others, we have explored various aspects of mental health, including stress management, overcoming biases, navigating workplace challenges, and fostering resilience. These narratives remind us that everyone has a story, and each experience offers a chance for growth, understanding, and connection.

Creating Supportive Work Environments

As leaders, colleagues, and organizations, it is crucial to create environments that prioritize mental health and well-being. Here are several actionable steps to consider:

1. **Foster Open Communication**: Encourage conversations about mental health and create a culture where employees feel safe discussing their challenges and seeking help.

2. **Implement Mental Health Programs**: Offer resources such as Employee Assistance Programs (EAPs), mental health days, and workshops on stress management and resilience.

3. **Promote Work-Life Balance**: Recognize the importance of balancing personal and professional commitments. Flexible work arrangements can lead to greater job satisfaction and productivity.

4. **Encourage Peer Support**: Establish peer support networks where employees can share their experiences, offer encouragement, and develop a sense of community.

5. **Educate on Mental Health**: Provide training for all employees, including management, to increase awareness of mental health issues and the importance of empathy and support in the workplace.

A Call to Action

As we conclude this book, I urge you to take action, whether as an individual or part of an organization. The stories you have read are not just cautionary tales but also guides to understanding and addressing mental health in the workplace. Here are some ways to apply the insights gained:

- **Reflect on Your Role**: Consider how you can contribute to a healthier work environment, whether by supporting a colleague, advocating for better policies, or engaging in self-care practices.

- **Share Your Story**: Your experiences can help others feel less alone. By sharing your journey, you can foster understanding and compassion among peers.

- **Commit to Continuous Learning**: Mental health is an evolving field. Stay informed about the latest research and practices to create a more supportive workplace.

Final Thoughts

Mental health should be a priority for everyone, transcending beyond those merely grappling with visible issues. It is crucial for cultivating a vibrant, innovative, and productive workplace. As we embark on our journeys, both individually and collectively, it is vital to recognize the importance of nurturing our mental well-being. Let us commit to transforming the narrative surrounding mental health in the workplace—from one characterized by silence and stigma to one rooted in openness, empathy, and support.

I am immensely grateful to have had the opportunity to share these stories and insights with you. They are not just narratives; they are reflections of our collective experiences, trials, and triumphs. Each story serves as a reminder that we are not alone in our struggles. Together, we can forge a future where every employee feels valued, understood, and empowered to thrive both personally and professionally.

In the profound words of Maya Angelou, "I've learned that people will forget what you said, people will forget what you did, but people will never forget how you made them feel." Let us take this to heart and strive to create environments where we uplift one another, where kindness and compassion are at the forefront of our interactions. Every small act of support can create ripples of positive change in the workplace.

I want to extend my deepest gratitude to you for joining me on this journey toward understanding and embracing mental health in the workplace. Together, we can build a better, more compassionate world of work, where mental health is prioritized, and each individual's well-being is valued. As we move forward, let us be advocates for change, voices of support, and champions of mental wellness.

May we foster a culture where every individual feels safe to express their concerns, seek help, and support their peers. By doing so, we can contribute to a world where everyone has the opportunity to flourish, not just survive. Thank you for being part of this vital conversation—together, we can pave the way for a brighter, healthier future in our workplaces and beyond.

Stay Connected

Thank you for joining me on this journey to explore workplace wellness and mental health. Your thoughts, experiences, and stories matter, and I'd love to hear from you!

If this book resonated with you, sparked new ideas, or helped you take steps toward a healthier and more balanced work life, please feel free to reach out. Whether you want to share your personal struggles, the coping strategies that have worked for you, or your thoughts on the book, your voice is important.

You can connect with me on:

- **Website:** iconnectway.com

- **Instagram:** @shruti.iconnect

- **LinkedIn:** Shruti Dey

- **YouTube:** @iconnect-counseling-therapy

For questions, feedback, or to share your stories, write to me at **shruti.dey@hotmail.com**. Who knows? Your journey and insights might inspire others as we continue to foster conversations about mental health in the workplace.

Let's keep the conversation going, break the stigma, and support each other in creating a world where mental health is prioritized, respected, and embraced.

Together, we can build a community that thrives on understanding, compassion, and resilience. Looking forward to hearing from you!

Warm regards,
Shruti Dey

Other Books by the Author

📖 *Magic in Me: 15 Stories of strength and positivity for Young Minds* – Inspiring bedtime stories read by parents or self-reading for children between age 5- 12 years.

www.ingramcontent.com/pod-product-compliance
Lightning Source LLC
Chambersburg PA
CBHW041329120726
48005CB00014B/2174